1

# Blessed

## *The Music and Ministry of The Imperials*

Rick L. Evans

Timothy D. Holder

Copyright 2025 by TDH Communications

Knoxville, TN

Cover Art Design by Jill Holder

Early Picture provided by Rick L. Evans

Later Pictures by Philip G. Brown Photography

ISBN 979-8-9866410-3-4

## Table of Contents

## Introduction

Rick L. Evans

The Imperials—their name has become iconic to many and is undoubtedly one of the foundational building blocks of contemporary Christian music (CCM). As a little boy, my dad took me to many Christian concerts, and like so many others, I sat in the front row, singing my heart out, dreaming of the day I would join so many of my musical heroes and proclaim God's words through music.

One of my first concerts featured Jim Murray, Armond Morales, Sherman Andrus, Joe Moscheo, and Terry Blackwood, AKA "The Imperials." I had never heard a more soul-searching sound before. The group was funny, relevant, and incredibly talented. Their music was a step above anything I had ever heard in the Christian marketplace, and after that first concert, I was hooked for life.

Growing up during the Jesus Movement in Southern California, all the new Christian music seemed to filter through the West Coast. I remember the controversy surrounding the new "rock" music and those who thought it would destroy the church and the American Christian experience. And, of course, The Imperials led the way to that path of perceived destruction.

Not only were the naysayers proved wrong about the impending destruction, but the group's legacy and music changed the industry and this little boy's life forever. After decades of travel and the privilege of being a part of the Billy Graham Evangelistic Association, the Harvest Crusade with Pastors Greg Laurie and Chuck Smith, and a member of Franklin Graham's festival team, my dream came true, and I became a member (and the general manager) of The Imperials.

Looking back through the years, I've discovered that the group's success has never been in one member or a particular song; instead, it is all in the team's "Call and Commission." The Imperials have always combined ministry with great songs and exquisite execution. The foundation of our success has been, and will always be, in the heartfelt delivery infused by God's leading and the group's desire to put Him first.

Not many groups can claim a 60+ year history of continuous successful music. Yet more important than our legacy or past accolades is the future that God has for us now to continue His call in our lives and the responsibility to fulfill the group's mission for future generations.

YES, The Imperials changed Christian music, remained relevant, and stayed ahead of the cultural curve with innovative approaches to sound and lyrics. Still, our most outstanding trophy is the lives that were changed along the way, including this little boy's life.

Timothy D. Holder

I remember when The Imperials first got on my radar. It was in the summer of 1982 during the World's Fair that was going on in Knoxville, Tennessee. Though I live in Knoxville today, back then, I grew up much further south in Winter Park, Florida. My church decided that my youth group should go to the World's Fair. I do not recall much of a spiritual emphasis on this youth trip, other than in the music we listened to. As we rode the bus there and back, one of the kids insisted that we play The Imperials' *Priority* album. The song "Trumpet of Jesus" was a particular hit with the youth group—myself included.

Shortly after we got back home, my oldest brother, Jim, got a copy of this album and played it.

A lot.

I loved *Priority*, but by the time I knew who they were, Russ Taff and his soulful voice had already left the group, and I remember being disappointed that there would never be another album quite like that one. I thought *the group just won't be the same.* Little did I know that The Imperials already had a bunch of excellent albums, that they would continue to make such albums for decades, or that I would be writing a book about them more than forty years later.

Looking back on it, I later realized that I had heard at least two Imperials songs before this World's Fair trip, and they were memorable enough that I still remember where I was when I heard them. Around 1976 or 1977, I was in the youth room at church, and the puppet ministry was a big thing (the '70s were a crazy time). Someone thought it would be a good idea to have the puppets pretend to sing The Imperials' hit "No Shortage." The person was right—it was a brilliant idea. The song was fun, the puppets pretending to sing it were funny, and it had a great message. A few years later, I walked into my parents' bedroom on a Sunday morning as we were getting ready to leave for church. The radio was on, and I heard "Praise the Lord." I literally stopped walking—I just stood there and listened. The vocals, the lyrics, and the music were so amazing, I wanted to focus on them to the exclusion of all else. I could not even move. I thought I was hearing the perfect song.

I do not know that I ever changed my mind.

As I said, it was only later that I connected those songs with The Imperials. The point is that their music was already a blessing to me before I even knew who they were.

For as much as I have appreciated various Imperials singers through the years, that appreciation is not limited to just their time in the group. *Walls of Glass* by Russ Taff is a fantastic album. The song "Silent Love" from his next release was a tremendous blessing when I struggled with spiritual doubt in college. *No Frills* by Paul Smith is another example of a great record by a former Imperial. My favorite album by the Gaither Vocal Band is *Wings*, which features Imperials alums Jim Murray and Gary McSpadden. That album also features the song "What Once was a River," written by David Robertson, who joined The Imperials two years after the Gaither Vocal Band recorded his song. Just a few years ago, I listened to *Stir It Up*, an Imperials release from 1992, and after I heard it, I went and ordered lead singer Jonathan Pierce's solo albums. And I know that countless other Imperials fans have some albums by former members that they love just as much as I do.

I have thoroughly enjoyed The Imperials over the years, and it is exciting for me that they are still doing great things. The Imperials album from 2023, "Blessed," is a really strong collection of songs. It is great to see Sherman Andrus, Terry Blackwood, Jim Murray, Russ Taff, Danny Ward, and others still out there making music and doing ministry.

The Imperials and their music have touched my life for years. I wanted to write this book to share that feeling with others. Interviewing these people and hearing their stories has been precious to me.

## Memories

Memories can indeed be complicated things, you know? It's incredible how our minds can sometimes play tricks on us when recalling events from the past. When details get a bit hazy or fuzzy in our memories, our imagination often fills those gaps. As much as we may not want to admit it, it's an undeniable truth.

That's why a tremendous amount of effort went into producing this book on the music and ministry of The Imperials, to ensure that it stays faithful to historical accuracy. The information within these pages came from Rick and Tim's extensive knowledge and firsthand experiences with the group, countless sources available in print and online, and over forty in-depth interviews that the authors conducted with singers, instrumentalists, producers, record company insiders, and many others closely associated with the band.

Even with all those resources at our disposal, we were still dealing with people accessing memories about events and music that sometimes dated back more than six decades. Recalling intricate details from that far in the past is no easy feat, no matter how vivid certain moments may have been.

Throughout this process, we did our absolute best to tell this story as faithfully and accurately as humanly possible, and we prayed that the Holy Spirit would guide us and provide us with the right words in any instances where our best efforts fell short.

This book is the culmination of that arduous yet rewarding journey. It is our sincere hope and prayer that the final product blesses you, the reader, and does justice to The Imperials' incredible legacy.

## Chapter 1

## The Beginning

## 1964-1965

### Jake Hess, Gary McSpadden, Armond Morales, Sherrill "Shaun" Neilsen, Henry Slaughter

*Jake Hess & The Imperials* (1964)
**Introducing the Illustrious Imperials** (1964)
*Fireside Hymns* (1964)
*Blends & Rhythms* (1964)
*Talent Times Five* (1965)
*Slaughter Writes–Imperials Sing* (1965)
*The Happy Sounds of Jake Hess & The Imperials* (1965)
*He Was a Preachin' Man* (1965)
*Slightly Regal* (1965)

 The origin story of The Imperials is relatively well-known. Jake Hess, a highly regarded southern gospel singer in the 1950s and 1960s, wanted to create a new group. He was not interested in auditioning strangers or simply filling slots with his friends; he wanted a group of all-stars. He also wanted more than just a collection of talented musicians who could sing southern gospel music. He envisioned a group that would do things differently when they performed—how they performed would be unique. But even that was not enough. He would insist that the men in his group sign a morals clause. He wanted to surround himself with people of character as well as talent. He did not want a group of guys who would just sing about the Lord—he thought it was important that their behavior and life matched the songs they sang.
 Jake had formed his vision of how things should be done from all his years in the southern gospel music

business, singing lead for the Statesmen Quartet (1948-1963), and he had dreamed of putting this super group together for years. One of the people with whom he discussed this was a woman who would eventually have a long-term and unique perspective on The Imperials, Brenda Nielsen Murray. She was married to The Imperials' first tenor, Sherrill Neilsen. Sherrill passed away in 2010, and in 2018, Brenda married Jim Murray, the second man to sing the high parts for the group. But her insider perspective was even greater than that. She said Jake had confided in her as early as 1960 or 1961 that he was considering creating this group.

While the group's start might be well-known, a lesser-known fact about its origin is that the foursome was initially a fivesome. Jake sang lead with three parts around him—Sherrill, often called "Shaun," Neilsen (tenor), Gary McSpadden (baritone), and Armond Morales (bass)—but the piano player, Henry Slaughter, was also considered a full-fledged member of the group.

All these men had impressive musical pedigrees. Jake first met Sherrill Neilsen when he was just four years old. Sherrill later won a vocal competition when he was thirteen. Just one year later, he was singing with the Speer Family.

Yes, you read that right, dear reader, Sherrill "Shaun" Neilsen was a professional, touring southern gospel singer at the tender age of fourteen.

After spending some time singing while a member of the US Air Force, Sherrill rejoined the Speers, which was the group he was with when Jake plucked him up.

Gary McSpadden was a member of the Oak Ridge Boys. After his stint with The Imperials, Gary would go on to become a part of the Bill Gaither Trio and the Gaither Vocal Band, as well as having an impressive solo career. He had put himself on the radar when he filled in for Jake when Jake needed to take some medical leave from the Statesmen.

Armond Morales and Henry Slaughter were with the Weatherford Quartet before joining The Imperials. When Jake recruited Armond, he had already logged more than a decade of professional singing experience. Armond and Jake could even do a little cross-promoting because Armond released an album in January 1964 called *The Gospel Voice of Armond Morales*.

Henry got his start with The Stamps Baxter Ozark Quartet before moving on to play piano for The Trumpeteers. He was a "quadruple threat" musically. He was the group's piano player but had started out in southern gospel music as a singer. The album *Slaughter Writes— Imperials Sing* was a testament to his songwriting ability. Finally, Henry did all the vocal arrangements on the first several albums the group put out. Even the first album after he left The Imperials featured Henry's arrangements.

Living out his dream, Jake and his team produced a prodigious number of albums in their first two years. Incredibly, the group released four albums in its first year of existence and five in their second year. Something that made this output a little more manageable was that it was not uncommon for these early albums to feature several songs that were shorter than the three-to-five-minute songs that would later become industry standards.

They started rehearsing in December 1963, and Jake wanted them to have plenty of albums to sell when they began touring. When they hit the road in 1964, they hit it hard. The group members were home for less than thirty days between concert dates that year.

The long tours were made easier when their first recording company, Benson Records, gave them a tour bus as a signing bonus. Little did they know they were contributing to another industry standard means of travel for gospel groups, i.e. The Bus.

Somehow, they also carved out enough time to sing on albums for several other people in this time, appearing on one such album in 1964 and three more in 1965. The Imperials sang backup on many albums over the next several years.

As mentioned earlier, Jake wanted his group to be different. The Imperials did not do encores—Jake was more interested in the message and sound than hype and showmanship. They were the first southern gospel group to give each singer his own individual microphone. Later, they were the first southern gospel group to go to wireless mics.

Steve Krampitz, who spent years as a Christian music disc jockey, is an expert on The Imperials. He became a fan in 1982 when friends introduced him to an Imperials album from years earlier, *Sail On*. Steve began collecting new releases from the group through the years, but he also went back and found all their earlier records. Today, Steve has a YouTube channel dedicated to contemporary Christian and southern gospel music that has 22,000 subscribers. Steve considers *Talent Times Five* to be the best Imperials' album of the 1960s. What Steve likes about it, besides the consistently stellar vocals, is that the album leans fully into stereo technology. Steve says that if you listen to the record with headphones, you can hear some sounds on the left and some on the right, which was cutting-edge technology back then. It provides a different musical experience than other music from that era.

When Imperials' legend Jim Murray was asked which Imperials' album from the 1960s was his favorite, he named one from this period, which was before he was a member of the group. Jim singled out *Slaughter Writes– Imperials Sing*. His wife, Brenda, had her own favorite from the 1960s, and it was also a 1965 release—*Slightly Regal*. In particular, she enjoyed the songs "Only Forever" and "Because He Loved Me."

One thing that brought the group some much needed exposure in these early years was AO Stinson signing them to a deal to appear on syndicated television. The Imperials had been based in Atlanta, Georgia, but their TV show would be recorded in Nashville and air Monday through Friday. This is what prompted The Imperials to move to Nashville.

According to Brenda, one of the fans of these TV appearances was Elvis Presley, who would get up early to watch the shows. His interest in the group would come to pay dividends they could not have fathomed in the mid-1960s.

Future Imperial Lonnie Ott remembers being at a venue with The Imperials when he was just a kid. He was there to perform in his family's trio, and while there, he was convinced he had just seen Elvis. It was actually Gary McSpadden.

After two years of hard work, the group faced its first transition: Shaun Neilsen left. It was a tough loss; Shaun's Irish tenor sound brought something special to The Imperials. But he found some of the group's structure to be a bit restrictive and thought his talents could take him elsewhere. He went on and spent many years singing with Elvis Presley. But his departure presented a real challenge in maintaining the quality of sound and expectation created by the group.

Despite this challenge and many more that would come, Jake pressed forward. He knew his group could continue doing extraordinary things.

**And The Imperials just kept singing**…

## Chapter 2

## The Beat Goes On

## 1966

### Jake Hess, Gary McSpadden, Armond Morales, Henry Slaughter, Jim Murray

### *The Imperials Sing Their Favorite Hymns*
### *The Imperials Sing Inspirational Classics*

With the departure of Shaun Neilsen, an opportunity was created. Jim Murray would be the first new guy to join the band. He had sung with four different southern gospel groups in a relatively short period, which gave him a lot of experience quickly. One of those groups was the Stamps Trio. Jim would work with the Stamps again on a tribute project about Elvis Presley many years later (as discussed later in this book). Despite bouncing around with the Stamps and other groups early on (The Melodaires, The Orrell Quartet, and Bob Wills and The Inspirations), The Imperials were such a good fit that Jim stayed with them for twenty years, and then he came back later.

Jim, who had sung his first solo in church at the tender age of six or seven, had caught Jake Hess's eye—or, more accurately, his ear—when Jake was first thinking about putting the group together. But in December 1963, when the group was first assembled, Jim was only nineteen. Thus, Shaun was picked. The point is that Jake was hardly disappointed in ending up with Jim, especially a slightly more seasoned Jim.

The group put out two albums in 1966, which would be a lot by later standards, but of course, it represented a slower pace for them than what they had done in both of the previous two years.

16

In 1966, The Imperials performed many concerts with other southern gospel groups, including Jake's old team, the Statesmen. It says something about him and them that there were no hard feelings despite his departure from them and the successful creation of his own singing group. The Imperials also performed at venues that were not traditional southern gospel habitats, displaying once again, as they so frequently did through the years, their creative approach to doing what they did.

Perhaps one of their more surprising performances was not in front of a crowd, but millions heard it. The Imperials sang multiple versions of the theme song of *Davy Crockett*, a television show that ran from 1964-1970. They did not sing the song's original version, but they sang the theme multiple times when it was rerecorded during the series' run.

Jake could not keep up with the heavy demands of touring because of health issues. He left the group, but he did not leave the Christian music industry behind. By 1968, he was back at it, singing and making new records. A decade later, Dallas Holm released the song "You and Me Jesus," written by Jake. Many years later, he enjoyed a renaissance as an active participant in Bill Gaither's Homecoming series.

Gary McSpadden and Henry Slaughter also left the group around this time. Gary spent the next decade as a church pastor before reentering the world of Christian music full-time. He later sang with the Gaither Vocal Band for years, and in the 1980s he co-hosted *PTL Today* after Jim Bakker was forced to leave the air because of multiple scandals.

Henry Slaughter went on to perform with his wife, Hazel, and he played with the Bill Gaither Trio in the 1970s. Henry wrote songs for many different recording artists, including Elvis Presley and Mahalia Jackson. He wrote more than two hundred songs and appeared on over twenty-five albums.

It is rather remarkable that Jake, Gary, and Henry's departure did not end The Imperials. In a way, though, their departures did lead to the end of The Imperials as people knew them. This southern gospel group would now begin a pivot into what would become something radically different.

Before Jake left, The Imperials were involved in a record project that should have won an award for the longest title for an album. The project was called *Doug Oldham with Jake Hess and The Imperials Sing Twelve Songs by Bill Gaither*. What a collection of musical talent. And...words. The album did not come out until 1967. Jake had already departed the group, and the remaining Imperials had to figure out what would come next.

**And The Imperials just kept singing...**

# Chapter 3

## The Trailblazers

### 1967-1970

**Armond Morales, Jim Murray, Joe Moscheo, Terry Blackwood, Roger Wiles**

*New Dimensions* (1968)
*Now* (1968)
*Love is the Thing* (1969)
*Gospel's Alive and Well* (1970)

In early 1967, Elvis Presley released a gospel music album entitled *How Great Thou Art*. He would eventually win a GRAMMY for it. The Imperials provided the background vocals on this release.

Despite that mountaintop experience, the departures of Gary McSpadden, Henry Slaughter, and especially Jake Hess sent a shockwave through the group. There was a shakeup in the leadership and chemistry of the team, but there was also a more immediate concern. Without Jake as the front man, eighty venues canceled their concerts. It's not surprising—Jake had built the group and was the driving force behind it.

Faced with this existential crisis, the reconstituted Imperials pressed forward behind their new lead singer. Fresh out of college, young Terry Blackwood helped define their new sound. He made his mark on the group not just with his vocals but with his vocal arrangements. He had grown up playing the piano, which gave him the musical wherewithal to assign parts to the guys. This was more the exception than the rule for southern gospel singers in this era. Many other groups just hashed out their parts informally as they practiced.

Terry didn't mind doing the extra work, nor did he particularly mind replacing a legend. Both tasks were easier than what he had been doing—selling ladies' shoes. You know what they say, adversity is a great teacher.

Future Imperial Sherman Andrus wrote of Terry in his autobiography, "He is a great singer, and he never got enough credit for his ability as a singer and an arranger."

Terry wasn't carrying the vocals single-handedly, though. Jim was still there, doing what he did, and he was quite impressed with the singing ability of their newest member, Roger Wiles, who was only twenty when he joined the group. By joining, the young baritone was able to fulfill his lifelong ambition of being a professional Christian singer.

Armond continued to strongly contribute to the group's vocals and guided the group to a different sound in this period, moving out from strictly southern gospel music and toward music with a broader appeal. As Armond said many years later while appearing on Mike Huckabee's television show, "My background was rooted in the big band scene. My experience was broader than just southern gospel music, and I felt that the Lord wanted us to offer music that appealed to a wider range of listeners."

On the piano, The Imperials now had Joe Moscheo taking over from Henry Slaughter. Joe had been an active figure in Christian music since the 1960s. He had played for the groups The Harmonies and The Prophets. In 1964, he released the album *The Piano Artistry of Joe Moscheo II and The Prophets Quartet.*

As The Imperials released four albums in these two years, it became evident to many listeners that they were becoming something a little different than the other southern gospel groups. They were evolving their sound to reach a broader audience while trying to stay true to their Christian roots.

The year 1968 marked a significant shift for The Imperials, as the premier southern gospel quartet. With the release of their album *New Dimensions*, they began to embrace a more contemporary, pop-oriented sound. This transition signaled to their dedicated listeners that the group was evolving, moving away from their traditional roots and exploring new musical territories.

While their earlier works had firmly established them as a force within the southern gospel genre, *New Dimensions* showcased a fresh, modern approach. The album's tracks featured catchy melodies, polished production, and a broader appeal that extended beyond their core fan base. This artistic evolution was a bold move, reflecting the changing musical landscape of the late 1960s.

For longtime fans of The Imperials' soulful harmonies and spiritual lyrics, the shift might have been a bit jarring at first. However, the group's unwavering talent and passion for their craft shone through, allowing them to seamlessly bridge the gap between their gospel roots and their newfound pop sensibilities.

As the years progressed, The Imperials continued to refine and expand their sound, blending various genres and influences into their unique musical tapestry. Their willingness to embrace change and experiment with new styles not only kept them relevant but also attracted a new generation of listeners, solidifying their legacy as trailblazers in the world of music.

As a musician, Greg Austin had been a longtime fan of The Imperials. He noted that on the seventh track of their album *New Dimensions*, titled "On the Other Side," the group truly captured the sound that would come to define who they were becoming. Greg remarked, "This album was groundbreaking. What The Imperials were known for was what they did behind the singer. This was a masterclass in how to back somebody up."

Greg credited Terry Blackwood and Roger Wiles for the distinctive sound The Imperials were creating. Their harmonies and background vocals were truly something special.

For Dan Ames, the song "A Thing Called Love" from the album *Now* made him a lifelong fan when he first heard it as a child listening to his parents' record. More importantly, The Imperials' ministry through music inspired Dan to pursue a similar path. He eventually became a worship leader, using music to spread the message of Hope through Christ.

One voice that particularly stood out to Dan was Jim Murray's. "I've always loved his pure tenor voice," Dan said. "It was purer than any I have ever heard. Jim's vocals had a clarity and smoothness that left a lasting impression".

In 1969, The Imperials' talent was recognized when they won the Dove Award for "Male Group of the Year". It would be the first of a dozen Dove Awards the group was blessed with over the years. A testament to their enduring artistry.

This particular lineup of The Imperials is the one that Larry Hall first remembers from his youth. A few years later, Larry had the opportunity to play keys for a group that opened for The Imperials on several occasions. Then, in the 1980s, Larry even filled in on keyboard for the group a couple of times when they were touring and needed a temporary replacement.

Armond Morales, The Imperials' bass singer and patriarch, had offered Larry a full-time position at one point. However, Larry had to decline as he was already committed to another band.

Before his professional music career took off, Larry was simply a kid who loved The Imperials' music. "I was intrigued by their vocal harmonies, and they appealed to my musical and spiritual sides. I didn't think of them as southern gospel. They were kind of jazz oriented, like the Lettermen and the Four Freshmen," Larry recalled.

Larry later got to know Armond and Jim personally by performing with them, but he was already impressed by their incredible voices. Regarding Armond, Larry felt he had "the best bass voice ever in terms of talent. He had the best bass voice in a quartet that I ever heard. Just smoothness, like butter."

And as for Jim, Larry gushed, "I was a huge fan of his singing. He had the smoothest tenor voice. It never got shrill or strained; it just floated above everything." Their vocals were truly something special.

For Larry, the album *Love is the Thing* stood out as a favorite from this era of The Imperials' discography. The harmonies and performances captured everything he loved about the group's sound.

## Innovators

The Imperials were incredibly prolific musicians during this era, producing album after album of catchy tunes. While their songs tended to be on the shorter side compared to their later work, you could sense a change starting to take place in their creative approach.

Take their hit "Bridge Over Troubled Water" from the *Gospel's Alive and Well* record - that was about as mainstream as you could get for the group at that point. It illuminated their gradual transition away from strictly traditional southern gospel towards a more secular-inspired tunes with positive and uplifting lyrics.

Jim Murray said, "We were learning how to introduce ministry in a way that people would receive it." Terry echoed that sentiment, saying, "We wanted to be different. Relate more to what the youth wanted to hear."

The 1969 album *Love is the Thing*, which even covered Stevie Wonder's "For Once in My Life," was a particular favorite of future Imperial Lonnie Ott. He felt it really "broke ground for Christian music" with its contemporary vibe.

However, perhaps their biggest game-changer was starting to collaborate with none other than Elvis Presley himself in July 1969. Elvis was a huge fan of the group and had them sing backup for his Las Vegas residencies. It was a career building opportunity, even though The Imperials already had a packed schedule of their own tours, gospel showcases, and "Jesus Music" festivals. Add to that their TV appearances - Carson, Douglas, Cavett, Bishop, and you have an already full itinerary.

They performed as Elvis's background vocalists for two years, singing on his GRAMMY-winning *He Touched Me* album and somehow managed to keep putting out their own new records during this whirlwind period, too.

Releases like 1969's *Gospel's Alive and Well*, with its hit "The First Day in Heaven," showed they weren't completely leaving their roots behind. It is worth noting that most every other southern gospel group past and present covered this song, certainly a testament to The Imperials' lasting influence in that realm.

So, while branching out creatively, they kept one foot in their traditional fanbase. It was certainly a transitional time as they strived to stay relevant without alienating their core supporters. It was a delicate balancing act that would set the stage for their continued reinvention in the years ahead.

**And The Imperials just kept singing…**

# Chapter 4

## Everything changes

### 1971

### Armond Morales, Jim Murray, Joe Moscheo, Terry Blackwood, Greg Gordon, Larry Gatlin

### *Time to Get It Together* (1971)

This part of The Imperial's journey marked an exciting new chapter for the band. It was uncharted territory and the next step into a world of possibilities. Each city, stage, and audience would add a new page to the epic tale of The Imperials' rise.

The Imperials had come a long way from their earliest days when Jake Hess was the driving force behind the group's success. Their association with Elvis Presley had certainly brought them attention. Still, by 1972, their GRAMMY nomination for the album *Time to Get It Together* proved they were a force to be reckoned with on their own merits. This groundbreaking record featured overtly Christian songs alongside pop hits like "My Sweet Lord" and "Let It Be" by the Beatles, infusing deeper spiritual meanings into secular tunes.

One of their biggest fans during this era was a young Bryan Duncan, who would later find fame with the Christian group Sweet Comfort Band and as a solo artist. "They were taking secular songs and putting them to a God message, or I guess a better way to say it is they were putting the gospel into secular songs. It was truly cutting edge. I had never heard that," Bryan raved, particularly admiring tracks like "Put Your Hand in the Hand" and their rendition of "Bridge Over Troubled Water."

After Roger Wiles departed, the group recruited the young and humorous Greg Gordon on baritone. Terry Blackwood fondly recalled Greg's "lighthearted, easy, and comical approach to life," like hiding on the bus to jump out and startle his bandmates after lunch stops. Though immensely talented, Greg eventually left due to The Imperials' grueling touring schedule as backup singers for other acts.

His replacement was Larry Gatlin, a gospel singer since childhood who put law school on hold to join the group in 1971. "Larry picked up the songs easily and did a great job," said Terry.

In addition to US-based concerts, The Imperials performed overseas that year and the next in places like Finland, where Allen Stenmark first saw them live after becoming a fan with their 1969 album *Love Is the Thing*. Remarkably, they sang entirely in English despite Finland's two official languages being Finnish and Swedish.

Back in the States, Larry departed for Nashville to pursue songwriting while the band was in Las Vegas. This decision paid off tremendously for him as Gatlin became an acclaimed songwriter for stars like Elvis, Glen Campbell, and Barbra Streisand. He formed the hit country group The Gatlin Brothers, scoring GRAMMYs and career-changing hits like "Broken Lady" and "All the Gold in California." One can't help but wonder how Larry's extended tenure might have impacted The Imperials' legacy.

Regardless, his exit paved the way for one of the group's most radical moves yet - a daring shift that would once again put them at the vanguard of Gospel Music in groundbreaking fashion.

**And The Imperials just kept singing…**

## Chapter 5

## The First Among Many Firsts

## 1972-1975

## Armond Morales, Jim Murray, Joe Moscheo, Terry Blackwood, Sherman Andrus

*Imperials* (1972)
*Live* (1973)
*Follow the Man with the Music* (1974)

In 1972, a pivotal moment occurred for The Imperials when Sherman Andrus joined the group, replacing Larry Gatlin. Sherman brought an impressive resume to the table, having released a solo album titled *I've Got Confidence* back in 1969. Before that, he had spent around seven years singing with Andrae Crouch and the Disciples, a renowned gospel group. However, Andrus left the Disciples because he wanted to spend less time on the road after his wife gave birth to their child. At this juncture, Sherman performed weekend concerts on his own and occasionally collaborated with other Christian artists on various music projects. He even briefly crossed paths with music giant Michael Martian, who later produced two albums for The Imperials.

Sherman found himself in this phase of life, juggling weekend performances and gig work with others, when he received the call from The Imperials. As it turned out, he knew Armond's sisters, and when an opening arose in the group, the sisters recommended Sherman's for the position.

Looking back, one might consider it a controversial, potentially even dangerous choice: a black man joining a southern gospel group in the early 1970s. His wife, understandably, questioned his decision to audition, but

Sherman's response was simple: "I've never been to Nashville. I wanted to see what it was like." So, he embarked on the trip to Nashville and auditioned for the group, driven by a desire to try something new and push his boundaries. Armond and Joe were impressed by what they heard and decided to give Sherman a chance.

Perhaps Armond's own Filipino heritage and Latino-sounding surname made him more open-minded about hiring a minority in that era than others might have been.

Sherman's addition to the team did indeed create some controversy. According to Jim Murray, they lost some bookings as a result. However, Jim remained steadfast, stating, "The Lord provided. We didn't go hungry. It didn't bother Armond; it didn't bother us. From the beginning, Jake had said, 'Let's be different.'"

The transition itself was a difficult, but Sherman was as well-equipped to handle this challenging opportunity as just about anyone could be. He had grown up in the segregated South, but he was a man who counted his blessings. He had loving parents and siblings, and the opportunity to make music had been a constant in his life. He recalls being in his first singing group, The Riverside Five, when he pulled together some classmates at the young age of nine or ten. The length of his consistent experience equipped him to handle this next chapter in his life.

According to Sherman, Andrae Crouch and the Disciples were more popular with white listeners than black audiences. Sherman, who sang lead for the group, said he was not so much a black gospel singer as a "crooner." Their group leaned more into a black gospel sound after Sherman left. This meant that Sherman was already comfortable with white audiences, and they were comfortable with him. Still, he might have worked too hard to fit in at first. He wanted to blend in, and he saw The Imperials as an excellent singing group, "the Gold Standard," as he put it, but not necessarily great performers. They did not put on a spectacle; it was all about the music. Armond and Joe were not initially comfortable with what they were getting from him, telling him, "We want more." Sherman looked back on those early days and admitted, "It was not entirely smooth. It wasn't easy." But as he began to be himself, things gradually improved within the group dynamic.

The challenges, however, extended far beyond just adapting to different singing styles and stage presence. In his autobiography, *My Story! His Song! Blessed!* Sherman recalled facing blatant racism during some early rehearsals, where attendants at some venues refused to believe he was part of the group. Even when dressed identically to the other members, the attendants remained skeptical. And it wasn't just venue employees - some audience members who came to watch the newly reconfigured group practice were visibly disturbed by the racial diversity, shaking their heads disapprovingly.

Sherman asserted his place by suggesting the group incorporate more personal testimonies and invitations to accept Christ into their concerts. Initially, Joe was hesitant, not out of hostility but uncertainty about whether such overt ministry would work in their industry. This innovative approach, however, would become a defining aspect that set The Imperials apart.

While the group had previously shared their faith on stage to some degree - Allan Stenmark recalled Joe leading a ministry talk when they toured Finland in 1971 – the group remained unsure about leaning into it as heavily as Sherman proposed. Ultimately, they gave it a chance, and Sherman spearheaded this brand new direction in gospel music...explicit ministry! When they returned to Finland the following year, Sherman had taken over that portion of the concert, and The Imperials became renowned for this extraordinary element.

"I wanted to impact other people's lives," said Sherman about his motivation. His exceptional talent had previously caught the attention of a secular record company, which hoped to sign him. Still, Sherman's passion was to excel in gospel music, singing praises to his Lord and sharing the message of Christ from the stage.

Those heartfelt testimonies and invitations for salvation would become a life-changing hallmark of The Imperials' performances. Armond would later reflect repeatedly that the altar calls Sherman introduced marked a profound spiritual transition for them all.

With Terry patiently teaching him the old songs note-by-note, Sherman steadily picked up the group's repertoire, and The Imperials found their new footing together.

Sherman Andrus was the newest member of The Imperials, and as such, he was paid the least. This posed a challenge since his wife and young son didn't immediately join him in Nashville. Thankfully, Sherman could supplement his income with some solo gigs on the side.

The Imperials were still doing backup vocals for other artists at the time, including Jimmy Dean, with whom they performed for two months each year in Las Vegas. Sherman witnessed to Jimmy multiple times. Though Sherman may not have gotten the spiritual result he hoped for, you have to admire his bold faith.

The group also sang backup for Carol Channing at various venues. What made that experience unique was that someone, certainly not one of The Imperials themselves, thought it would be a great idea for them to do choreography. The Imperials were never excellent dancers, but at least they got plenty of laughs.

They additionally had the opportunity to tour with and open for Pat Boone during this period.

Though The Imperials were no longer singing backup for Elvis Presley in concerts, their relationship with him continued. Elvis liked to gather musicians after his shows and sing through the night. The Imperials would sometimes join him after an evening of performing with Jimmy Dean. According to Sherman, Elvis didn't just sing gospel music, but he really enjoyed it when he did. They sang more gospel than rock during these late-night sing-alongs, sometimes going until 7 am.

As mentioned earlier, The Imperials provided backup vocals on another Elvis album in 1972 called *He Touched Me*, featuring six songs they had already released. The album was another GRAMMY winner for Elvis, thanks in part to The Imperials' contributions.

During these years, The Imperials released three of their own albums. The first, self-titled *The Imperials*, was the least commercially successful of the Andrus and Blackwood era. Several tracks were mainstream songs, with "Gospel Ship" being a notable exception. It was an interesting time for the group. They had their own concerts, their own recording schedule, the time and commitment singing backup for secular artists, and performing songs written by industry superstars like names like Stevie Wonder, Carole King, and Kris Kristofferson.

Without a defined direction, the group was no longer billing itself as a southern gospel group at this point. Their reputation for performing different genres - contemporary, pop, country, and gospel - was just another reason why Sherman felt they needed to put more spiritual emphasis in their concerts. The group believed that they could sing what they wanted, but they had to stand for what they believed. o The Imperials began to define their ultimate purpose and calling.

Their next album, *Live*, would become the group's second GRAMMY-nominated work and their most popular of the Andrus/Blackwood era. Its three biggest songs showcased something that's made The Imperials special - different lead vocalists. Terry led "Light at the End of the Darkness," Jim sang his second most popular song of this era after "Bridge Over Troubled Water" with "More Than You'll

Ever Know," and Sherman was the featured voice on "Jesus Made Me Higher."

One of the things that resonated with Christian music DJ Steve Krampitz about the *Live* double album was The Imperials' unapologetic and unwavering commitment to their faith. Despite achieving tremendous success as backup vocalists for mainstream artists and their own recordings of some secular songs, The Imperials never wavered in their desire to communicate their Christian beliefs. What Krampitz found particularly powerful was that the *Live* album didn't just showcase The Imperials' impressive vocal talents – it served as a bold declaration of their spiritual convictions. The album culminated with an altar call, inviting listeners to make a personal commitment to Christianity. In Krampitz's view, this willingness to share The Gospel message so transparently, even at the peak of their mainstream popularity, was a testament to The Imperials' integrity and devotion.

For Krampitz, the *Live* album wasn't just a collection of great songs – it was a poignant reminder that even amidst the glitz and glamor of the entertainment industry, The Imperials remained steadfastly grounded in their faith. Their commitment to using their platform to spread the Word resonated deeply with Krampitz and countless other Christian music fans who appreciated the group's unwavering spiritual authenticity.

The *Live* album was Keith Thomas' favorite. Keith would later work with The Imperials on multiple albums in the 1980s as well as a vast array of stars, including Amy Grant, Vanessa Williams, James Ingram, BeBe and CeCe Winans, and many others. In high school, in the early 1970s, Keith had a band called "Sonshine" that patterned itself after The Imperials. In particular, Keith was impressed by Terry Blackwood. According to Keith, "Terry had a way of singing that went to the heart. I loved his voice. I loved how he carried himself."

It was during this time period, around 1973, when future Christian recording artist Bryan Duncan first saw The Imperials live. Can you imagine being a young kid and seeing your musical heroes perform live for the first time? That's exactly what happened to Bryan. It was at a venue that held about six hundred people, and it was packed to the brim. Bryan said, "Vocally, they were bigger than life." Their powerful vocals must have blown him away as a budding musician.

Bryan would later cross paths with members of the group during his long and successful career in contemporary Christian music. Although their interactions were fairly casual, just saying hello in hotel lobbies, it still left an impression on Bryan. He said, "They were casual. You wouldn't know they were stars." It's always cool when famous musicians remain down-to-earth despite their celebrity status.

After the *Follow the Man with the Music* release, Joe Moscheo stopped playing with the group but did not leave The Imperials behind completely. He stayed involved with them in a leadership position for a while. This shows how tight-knit the group was - even after members departed, they maintained close connections.

Joe went on to be an executive for New Direction Artist Guild in the 1970s, and by 1980, he was the vice president of BMI. BMI stands for "Broadcast Music, Incorporated." It is the organization that makes sure songwriters and publishers get paid when their works are performed. BMI looks after the interests of hundreds of thousands of people, so it is seriously impressive that Joe was able to rise to such a prominent leadership position in the organization. His career trajectory is admirable.

Another interesting fact is that back in the 1970s, during the ministry of this collection of The Imperials, Rick Evans, future general manager of and singer with the group, saw them for the first time and became a lifelong fan. His dad told him, "Someday, you will be up there." Can you imagine having that kind of foresight about your child's future? Little did Rick know how prophetic his dad's words would be. Rick's story is a heartwarming journey of a dream realized through hard work and perseverance.

In the end, Sherman Andrus's addition to The Imperials proved groundbreaking and ultimately successful, despite the initial challenges and controversies. His unique background and talent helped shape the group's sound and paved the way for greater inclusivity in southern gospel music.

**And The Imperials just kept singing…**

## Chapter 6

## Far From Their Roots

## 1975-1976

## Armond Morales, Jim Murray, Terry Blackwood, Sherman Andrus

*No Shortage* (1975)
*Just Because* (1976)

Sherman Andrus and Terry Blackwood were the driving forces behind The Imperials' shift towards a more contemporary sound on their 1975 album *No Shortage*. As the album's sales surpassed 50,000 units, the group deservedly felt they had achieved a rare success. *No Shortage* would become their first GRAMMY-winning album, earning them a Dove Award for "Male Group of the Year" in 1976. Remarkably, the album even won the Dove for "Pop/Contemporary Album of the Year" that year, signaling The Imperials' complete departure from their southern gospel roots, even before the arrivals of Russ Taff and David Will.

Keyboardist Larry Hall, who would later join The Imperials on tour and enjoy a successful career playing for various artists, fondly recalls *No Shortage* as "a definite step up to a more contemporary, funky sound. It was in the vein of what the Bee Gees were doing." The album also left a lasting impression on Mel Tunney, who sang with the Christian groups Truth and First Call. When she joined Truth, they were performing their own arrangements of Imperial's songs, and she cherished the opportunity to perform tracks like "Would You Believe in Me" and "No Shortage," as she thoroughly enjoyed listening to them on The Imperials' award-winning album.

Long-time Imperial fan Allan Stenmark cites *No Shortage* as his favorite album, with "Light at the End of the Darkness" being his standout track. The group's follow-up, *Just Because*, earned another GRAMMY nomination and was a particular favorite of Neal Joseph, who would later produce multiple Imperials albums in the 1980s. Mel Tunney was also a big fan of *Just Because*, especially the title track.

*Just Because* marked the final album featuring the dynamic duo of Andrus and Blackwood. While The Imperials were thriving in the mid-1970s, change was on the horizon. Blackwood had lost his father in 1974, and by 1976, he felt the need to spend less time on the road to assist his mother. However, he remained committed to making music for the Lord and was willing to tour, albeit less frequently.

After nine years as an integral part of The Imperials, Blackwood reflected, "I had a great relationship with the guys." Regarding their efforts to live out the messages they sang on stage, he added, "No one wanted friction on the bus. We wanted to be consistent in our faith."

Andrus and Blackwood's voices blended seamlessly. Long-time listener Phil Brown noted, "Their voices complemented each other well. Sometimes people would hear their music and say, 'I'm not sure if that's Terry or Sherman.'" This phenomenon would later occur with David Will, Jim Murray, and others whose distinctive voices could occasionally switch parts due to their overlapping ranges. While this could confuse some listeners with less discerning ears, it ultimately contributed to The Imperials' rich, harmonious sound.

Terry Blackwood wasn't running away from The Imperials but towards something else. He wasn't tired of the group, he simply needed to be more available for his family for a while. After leaving The Imperials, Terry teamed up with his sister Kaye to record the album *All Things Work Together*. While touring to promote that record, he received an invitation to visit India, which he accepted. It was there that Terry had the incredible honor of meeting Mother Teresa.

Not long after Terry's departure, Sherman Andrus also left The Imperials for the same reason - to spend less time on the road and more time at home with loved ones. Sometime after returning to the States, Terry was approached by executives at Benson Records with an intriguing proposition. They believed Terry and Sherman could put together their own successful group. Terry called Sherman, and after some convincing, the two former Imperials agreed to give it a shot.

After spending nine years with The Imperials, Terry spent roughly another nine years as part of the group ", Blackwood, and Company. They released seven albums together, including a greatest hits compilation, before disbanding in the mid-1980s. Sherman and Terry never expected to end up in a second group together. Still, the record label had assured them their involvement could be fairly minimal - make the music and do some light promotion. However, once their debut album dropped and the realization of its possible success began to his the executives, the label pushed the guys to hit the road.

Despite the unexpected road work, Sherman and Terry ran the group well together. Both men were ministry-minded with easygoing personalities. And having never been in official leadership roles with The Imperials, they were sensitive to the feelings of non-decision makers in their new group. After Andrus, Blackwood, and Company's run ended, the two friends continued making music for the Lord, eventually reuniting with their former quartet mates in The Imperials years later. Sherman also released three albums with singer Lonny Bingle, who had previously recorded a solo project produced by Terry.

For his part, Terry has been incredibly active over the decades, recording solo albums and with various other groups. He's also participated in many popular Gaither Homecoming projects celebrating southern gospel's rich heritage.

Meanwhile in The Imperials' camp, could the group survive losing Sherman Andrus and Terry Blackwood? Their future was quite uncertain. The group had been pushing the boundaries of southern gospel for years, and they weren't yet fully embraced as a pop/contemporary act despite a Dove Award in that category. Could Armond Morales and Jim Murray take The Imperials even further into the brave new world of contemporary Christian music? And should they even try without the beloved Andrus and Blackwood leading the group vocally? These were precarious times indeed for the legendary quartet.

**And The Imperials just kept singing**…

## Chapter 7

## You Will Never Believe What The Imperials Did

## 1976-1981

## Armond Morales, Jim Murray, David Will, Russ Taff

**The Lost Album** (The album was recorded in 1976 and
1977 but released in 2006)
*Sail On* (1977)
*Imperials Live* (1978)
*Heed the Call* (1979)
*One More Song for You* (1979)
*Priority* (1980)
*Christmas with The Imperials* (1980)
*The Very Best of The Imperials* (1981)

The Imperials underwent significant lineup changes
in the mid-1970s that would shape the group's sound and
direction for years to come. In 1976, David Will and Russ
Taff joined the iconic Christian music group, ushering in a
new era.

David Will was the first to come aboard after Terry
Blackwood's departure. David had spent years singing
southern gospel with groups like the Keystones Quartet, The
Statesmen, and The Tribunes. Like many of his counterparts,
David was deeply rooted in ministry - he was a licensed
minister before becoming a professional musician.

The story of how David joined The Imperials is
unique. He attended one of their concerts when he was
unexpectedly asked to sing during intermission. Armond
Morales, the group's founder, was so impressed that he
invited David to join the group right then and there.

Not long after, Russ Taff replaced Sherman Andrus.
Russ had been part of the band Sounds of Joy with his friend

James Hollihan Jr. Even from a young age, Russ displayed incredible vocal talent, singing at church as a little boy.

His time with Sounds of Joy helped prepare Russ both spiritually and musically for his future with The Imperials. James recounted, "We would just set up in a park and play. People would go out on the streets and share about Jesus. Everything was about evangelizing and ministering. If we were going somewhere to perform, and we saw someone on the side of the road with a flat tire, we would stop and pray for them and help them change their tire. We were spreading the Word."

Russ's big break came in 1974 when Sounds of Joy opened for The Imperials, planting the seeds for his audition two years later. Between leaving Sounds of Joy and joining The Imperials, Russ worked with evangelist Jerry Savelle, singing and leading worship at his events. When The Imperials opportunity arose, Jerry encouraged Russ to pray about it, which he did before accepting.

Speaking of major life events, Russ had recently proposed to his girlfriend Tori, who happily accepted. However, their planned wedding date conflicted with The Imperials' touring schedule. With few options, they settled on October 31, 1976. They had their wedding on Halloween. Tori joked that at least no one would forget their anniversary.

With David and Russ on board, The Imperials embraced a new sound that blended their southern gospel roots with contemporary Christian music styles. Their label, Word Records, even created a new imprint called DaySpring specifically for the evolving group. It was the start of an exciting new chapter.

It was an intriguing turn of events that had led Russ Taff to audition for The Imperials. Joe Moscheo, who had previously played piano for the group but was now their manager, reached out to Russ with a phone call inviting him to try out.

At just 22 years old, Russ joined the legendary quartet. When they needed a bass guitarist, Russ and Armond Morales brought in James Hollihan Jr., who carved out a niche playing bass on tour and writing a few tunes for them. Once the lead guitarist departed, James transitioned to that role. After his stint with The Imperials, James enjoyed a successful career as a musician, songwriter, and producer.

By the time Russ eventually left the group years later, he had taken the lead on several hit songs for The Imperials. His replacements certainly had massive shoes to fill. Ironically, Russ understood that feeling well, having initially stepped in for the iconic Sherman Andrus. As Russ recounted in his memoir *I Still Believe*, there were several Andrus-led songs the group wanted to perform, but Russ preferred not to sing lead on most of them out of deference to Sherman. The soulful-voiced Russ seemed a natural fit, but he only took over lead vocals on "He Looked Beyond My Faults," with Dave Will and Jim Murray handling the other Andrus tunes.

Russ appreciated Armond's and Jim's patience as he found his footing in those early days. As the owners, they gave him space to develop his sound, though Dave was also supportive during the transition.

Vocally, Russ proved to be a game-changer for The Imperials. As Christian artist Chris Christian wrote, Russ was "dynamic" and "could make an average song good and a great song a hit." Fellow singer Jeoffrey Benward echoed that sentiment: "I'm much like every other contemporary Christian singer. We all wanted to sound like Russ Taff." Jeoffrey, who released three solo albums and three more with his son Aaron, did bear some vocal resemblance to Russ.

The first album from this new Imperials lineup was produced by the talented Gary S. Paxton, Bob McKenzie, and former Imperial Joe Moscheo. Interestingly, Armond

41

recalled that Gary insisted on a bizarre diet of canned cold spinach during the recording sessions.

Despite the impressive talents of Russ and Dave Will, the album failed to meet the label's expectations. *The Lost Album* sat on the shelves for three decades before finally being released, mixing contemporary sounds with southern gospel and 1970s folk styles. While not their most significant commercial success, it was treasured by longtime fans. Industry veteran Stan Moser explained it simply wasn't the new direction Word Records wanted for the group.

Indeed, The Imperials would soon embrace the emerging "contemporary Christian music" genre that perfectly suited Russ's soulful vocals. However, not everyone initially saw Russ as the ideal successor to Sherman Andrus and Terry Blackwood's revered era. Rick Evans, current GM of the group, admitted that after seeing Russ perform early on, he told friends, "This guy will never replace Sherman or Terry." Rick now admits that he missed that one by a mile….

However, The Imperials were about to reach new heights, and their impact would extend far beyond music. At an early 1977 concert, Stan Moser, then a Christian music executive, had a life-changing spiritual awakening while Dave Will shared about hope from the stage. It was one of countless examples of The Imperials using their platform to share their faith, carrying on Sherman Andrus' vision for ministry.

Rick Evans vividly recalled Russ singing at a Disneyland performance and that the group shared the message of Jesus with those who needed to hear. The Imperials were certainly using their platform to accomplish their ministry purpose.

According to James Hollihan, Russ Taff would usually preach before one of his songs, and David Will would offer some kind of invitation near the end of their concerts.

Chris Christian came on board to produce multiple Imperials albums during this era. Describing their time in the studio together, he said, "We were there to make music to go around the world and touch people for Jesus. We weren't doing it for the GRAMMYs. We were praying that God would use us." His perspective highlights their pure motives and desire to spread the gospel through their music.

Chris enjoyed working with each of the four group members, who were still getting to know each other at that point. He found them all nice guys who worked well together and collaborated smoothly with him as the producer. Musically, they could all handle lead vocal parts when called upon, and they each had unique strengths. Russ's vocals were extraordinary. Jim Murray had a great tenor voice and a commanding stage presence too. David Will was a skilled harmonizer, and Armond Morales was the glue that helped unify and hold everything together.

Their commercial success grew rapidly. They went from selling around 50,000 units of their previous album *No Shortage*—which was considered quite a good number at the time according to Stan Moser—to moving over 300,000 copies with the *Sail On* album. The reasons for the *Sail On* project to runaway success were clear—it simply contained so many outstanding songs.

Jim Murray's soaring tenor voice propelled hits like the title track "Sail On," which reached #3 on the Adult Contemporary Christian radio charts, and "Bread on the Water." The song "Sail On" would become Jim's favorite from all his years with The Imperials. Producer Chris Christian had the honor of writing this signature song and producing the entire album. He attended the GRAMMY Awards ceremony that year when The Imperials got to perform "Sail On" live. While backstage at the event, Chris found himself in an impromptu conversation with the legendary Bob Dylan. When Dylan learned that Chris was there because of "Sail On," the iconic singer-songwriter started belting out the lyrics on the spot, clearly a fan.

The story behind the writing of "Sail On" is also quite fun. Stan Moser had signed The Imperials to his WORD label. Stan was ready to launch a full-scale marketing push for a big hit record, with all the pieces in place...except for the actual hit record. Producer Chris Christian was given just five weeks to deliver a "masterpiece," but he also promised his wife a pre-scheduled beach vacation. So, the Christian family went on their beach trip, and each morning Chris got up early with his guitar and prayed for inspiration. He was sitting there watching sailboats go by when the iconic melody and lyrics for "Sail On" came to him in about eight minutes of writing. He said, "It seemed like a great vehicle for Jim's voice and offered a nice counterpart for Armond to stand out on."

The other songs on the album then came together quickly out of necessity. Jim co-wrote "Sonlight" with guitarist James Hollihan as they rode on the bus between concert dates. Russ contributed the album's closing song, "Try Again."

This new lineup of The Imperials had departed from the group's southern gospel roots. As Chris Christian explained, "I had no background in that type of music. I had not listened to it, and I did not know it. And there was no term for contemporary Christian music yet. There was gospel music, and some Christians made music with a more mainstream sound. I went into the world to share the gospel through pop music." That contemporary pop/rock style was the sound he knew how to produce.

What would truly signify the new musical direction for this Imperials era was the opening song on the *Sail On* album called "Water Grave," featuring Russ Taff on lead vocals. It was a soulful-sounding, legitimate rock song that showcased what Russ and the whole group were capable of in this innovative genre.

For Chris Hauser, who would become a significant figure in Christian radio and the music industry, hearing "Water Grave" was initially quite a shock. He loved secular rock music but had never heard anything like that with spiritual lyrics until this

Renowned guitarist Tom Hemby's journey with The Imperials began in 1978 when he attended one of their concerts. Tom and his wife were considering leaving early that night due to their young daughter, but Larry Hall, the keyboardist for the opening act, persuaded them to stay. Larry had heard that The Imperials' guitar player was leaving and thought Tom should stick around to meet Armond.

Tom was introduced to Armond, who auditioned him on the spot. Tom, a future multiple Dove Award and GRAMMY winner, initially played bass guitar for the group because James Hollihan had decided to switch from bass to lead guitar. A few years later, when James left, Tom took over on lead guitar.

Looking back, Tom fondly recalled, "There were a lot of great moments in my time with the group. The relationships with the guys were pretty special."

Meanwhile, The Imperials continued their momentum with the album Heed the Call, produced by Chris Christian, who also wrote the title track. Stan identified "Praise the Lord" and "Oh Buddha" as the breakout hits, with Russ taking the lead vocals on both songs that became enduring classics and concert favorites.

Interestingly, Chris clarified that songs like "Oh Buddha" and "First Morning in Heaven" were not attempts to appeal to their older southern gospel fans, as again, he did not have a background in that genre. "My background before I got into producing was writing jingles. I saw "Oh Buddha" as a novelty song," Chris explained.

Regardless of his intent, "Oh Buddha" became a hit in concerts and topped the Contemporary, Inspirational, and southern gospel charts. Though creating a southern gospel sound was not Chris's goal, he inadvertently achieved that mark.

"Praise the Lord" won the Dove Award for "Song of the Year" in 1980 and was recognized as the 67th greatest song in Contemporary Christian music over roughly thirty years by the editors of CCM Magazine. Remarkably, in a 1998 poll, "Praise the Lord" was voted one of the 10 best contemporary Christian songs of all time.

Chris Christian sat speechless in the studio after finishing recording "Praise the Lord" at 4:30 in the morning, knowing they had created something truly special. He later said, "'Praise the Lord' will outlive most of us."

Tim Holder, a long-time fan, shared a profound memory: "I remember the first time I heard 'Praise the Lord.' It was more than forty years ago on a Sunday morning. I had walked into my parents' bedroom for something, and as I was walking out, this song came on the radio. The lyrics, the vocals, and the music were just overwhelming. I was frozen in my tracks, mesmerized. I had never realized that a song could be that good. It was a blessing, then, and it has continued to be one over the years."

For Chris, another standout track from *Heed the Call* was "Overcomer," written by James Hollihan, which he described as a true gem.

*Heed the Call* marked a shift for The Imperials, with the first four songs featuring Russ Taff on lead vocals and the group providing backup. Russ also sang lead on two other tracks, while Jim and Dave each had two solo features, leaving one for Armond. With his exceptional talent, Russ had become the dominant voice of the group.

Long-time fan Dan Ames shared, "I played that album until it couldn't be played anymore. Every word just spoke to me."

In 2024, when asked who he would like to work with again if given the chance, Chris Christian named BJ Thomas and The Imperials.

In the late 1970s, The Imperials began booking concerts outside of churches and in arenas that could accommodate up to 10,000 people, a rarity in Christian music at the time. James Hollihan estimated they were on tour for a couple hundred days out of the year, a significant commitment but less demanding than their mid-1960s schedule.

The success of *Heed the Call*, particularly Russ's vocal prowess, caught the attention of producer Michael Omartian, who was blown away by "Praise the Lord." Michael, on the cusp of becoming a major figure as a music producer after winning three GRAMMYs for Christopher Cross's self-titled debut album in 1979, was eager to collaborate with The Imperials.

Recording an album in just 29 days was no easy feat, especially back in those days when most albums took three to six months to complete. But that's exactly what Michael Omartian and The Imperials accomplished with *One More Song for You.*

Michael's wife, Stormie, co-wrote several songs on both albums her husband produced for The Imperials, laying the foundation for her future success as an author with books like *The Power of a Praying Wife* and its subsequent series. While Russ Taff dominated vocally on most tracks, Armond Morales didn't mind taking a backseat, content to focus on leading people to Christ through the powerful altar calls.

As Michael recalled, "It was never about ego with any of these guys." Even Jim Murray, initially reluctant to embrace the contemporary sound, eventually came around thanks to Michael's encouragement and creative vision. Looking back, Jim admitted, "He was so good, so creative. We were blessed to have him." Highlights from the Omartian-produced albums included the Russ Taff-led hits

"Trumpet of Jesus" and "Praise the Lord," as well as the poignant "One More Song for You," penned specifically for David Will.

For bassist Tom Hemby, a career highlight was co-writing "Living Without Your Love," showcasing Jim Murray's vocals. Years later, and after he was no longer in the group, Tom's "Power of God" made it onto the fun album *This Year's Model*. But it wasn't just the music that made an impact – Tom fondly recalled the laughter and pranks that came with life on the road, from cheating at cards to shaving cream attacks on unsuspecting soundmen.

As the 70s drew to a close, Russ Taff's star power propelled the group to new heights, with Tom Reeves witnessing "busses from fifty different churches" and "thousands coming down front during the altar call." Future Imperials singer Danny Ward likened their concerts to "the circus coming to town, but in a good way," where fans expected to witness "amazing things."

It was an incredible time for The Imperials, with their music soaring to new heights of popularity and acclaim. Their second album produced by Michael Omartian, *Priority*, capped off an amazing run, earning a GRAMMY alongside two previous GRAMMY wins for *Sail On* and *Heed the Call*. From 1978 to 1981, the group dominated the Dove Awards, taking home five trophies, with *Priority* earning yet another Dove in 1982 after Russ Taff had departed.

The Imperials' impact extended far beyond awards and sales figures. In 1980, a young man named Barry Weeks attended one of their concerts in Roanoke, Virginia while on a date with his future wife. Though involved in music from a young age and serious about his faith, Barry had never experienced Christian music like The Imperials' performance. "I loved it!" He said to his girlfriend, "I could sing in that group. I could do that." And as fate would have it, Barry did indeed join The Imperials a few years later, appearing on one album and producing two more.

For the quartet of Russ Taff, Armond Morales, Jim Murray, and Dave Will, that time represented some of the most outstanding years for the group, though it was never without challenges. As Russ recalled, "We were performing at the GRAMMYs on one hand, and on the other, we had to drive our tour bus from concert to concert. Being the youngest, I drew the short straw – I might have to drive from 1 AM to 7 AM after an evening show."

The pristine production values of *Priority* struck a chord with listeners. Chris Hauser, a Christian radio veteran, reflected, "It had a clearer, more pristine production than other records. It was so celebratory, triumphant, and happy." The Imperials' music became Chris's constant companion during that era. Fellow singer Jeoffrey Benward was "blown away by the production and Russ's voice" upon *Priority*'s release.

In Chris Hauser's estimation, the Russ Taff years represented an "explosive" period for the entire Christian music industry. "What Russ, Armond, Jim, and Dave did at that time was not just big for The Imperials but for contemporary Christian music."

The Imperials' impact extended beyond the studio of course. In late 1980, Dick Tunney joined their touring band on keyboards, having previously played with the opening act Truth. For Dick and his wife Mel, it was a dream come true – they saw The Imperials as "the gold standard in Christian music" at that time. The Tunneys also appreciated the group's family-friendly policies, allowing spouses to join their husbands on tour.

One particularly memorable tour stop came around January 20, 1981, when the group performed at an inaugural ball celebrating the presidency of Ronald Reagan in Washington, D.C.

The group's Christmas album from the Russ Taff era showcased more evenly distributed vocals among Russ, Jim, and David, with a rare duet between Russ and Armond on "Silent Night." Though less pop-oriented than their other releases, the record still sounded fantastic, including a jazzy big-band number that foreshadowed Russ's first future solo Christmas album.

After leaving The Imperials, Russ went on to achieve tremendous solo success with numerous awards and bestselling albums. His debut solo record, *Walls of Glass*, was produced by multi-Grammy winner Bill Schnee, who would also produce two Imperials albums. Bill called Russ "one of the most soulful singers in any genre."

Russ Taff's musical journey has been nothing short of remarkable. His first six solo albums soared to the top of the Christian music charts, with hits like "We Will Stand" and "Medals" becoming anthems of the mid-1980s. The book *100 Greatest Songs in Christian Music* ranked "We Will Stand" as #29 on their prestigious list.

Larry Hall, who toured with Russ for years and worked on several of his albums, cited *Walls of Glass* and the later release *Faroe Islands* as standout efforts, noting that the latter features "some phenomenal songs." Russ's rendition of the "Day by Day" hymn from *Faroe Islands* is undoubtedly among his finest works.

Through it all, Russ Taff's unwavering commitment to artistic growth and his willingness to embrace change have made him a true icon of Christian music.

**And The Imperials just kept singing…**

# Chapter 8

## A True Professional: Paul Smith

### 1981-1985

### Armond Morales, Jim Murray, David Will, Paul Smith

*Stand by the Power* (1982)
*Side by Side* (1983)
*The Imperials Sing the Classics* (1984)
*Let the Wind Blow* (1985)

The next chapter in the life of The Imperials is one of the most impressive in CCM history. How do you replace a true icon and continue an unprecedented reign of excellence and success? The answer was Paul Smith.

The music world was buzzing about how The Imperials would move forward after Russ Taff's exit. Many articles tried to help The Imperials find their way, with some speculating that Paul was brought in specifically because he could cover the parts Russ sang. In contrast, others said he would bring a different sound altogether. The talk around Nashville was diverse and skeptical about whether this new lineup could recapture the magic.

When asked about his role, Paul said he hoped to strike a balance. "I was supposed to cover Russ's songs, but I was also tasked to strike a different flavor to a familiar sound." It was a tall order, but one he was determined to meet.

Longtime Imperials fan Dan Ames admitted his initial skepticism. "Did I want to allow Paul to impress me? Because of Russ, no, I didn't. But then I heard him and realized he brought a whole new sound. And I thought 'Wow, he can hit any note he wants.'" Dick and Mel Tunney, who worked closely with the group, shared Dan's initial doubts but quickly came around to appreciating Paul's talents. As Dick put it, "Paul was put in an incredibly difficult position. Russ sang many of the big songs they had. You didn't want to hear anybody else sing them." But Mel pointed out, "Paul carved a niche. Paul made his place." Soon, the group was back winning awards and shattering expectations.

What helped Paul succeed, besides his immense vocal skills, was his humility and spiritual focus. As Dick noted, "He made that place with his songwriting. Paul's fingerprints are all over those songs. It took some real fortitude, and Paul had it." But Paul saw his music career not as a quest for stardom but simply as his "calling to ministry."

The Tunneys had high praise for the other members, too. Of Armond Morales, Mel said "He was a man of few words. He had a ministry heart. I enjoyed working for him." Jim Murray earned raves for his "strong, amazing voice" and ability to convey his heart through ballads. As Dick put it, "Jim's voice was so clear. It was just a beautiful tone." And Dave Will brought an everyman quality, with Mel describing him as "the most regular guy—he was relatable. The other guys had more stage experience, but Dave brought an approachability."

This new lineup gelled, overcame the skeptics in a very short time, and captured the next season of The Imperials' amazing story through their talents, humility, and devotion to ministry.

Dick Tunney was among the many individuals who marveled at Dave Wills' extraordinary ability to fix anything on the bus. Dick likened him to a Swiss army knife. Whether working on the bus, recording a hit song, or simply traveling with the group, Dave was an integral part that kept the famous foursome functioning smoothly.

Now, let's delve into Paul Smith's captivating story: It was an exhilarating whirlwind when he joined the renowned Christian music group, The Imperials. At that time, Paul was already making waves as a solo artist and promoter of Christian music concerts. Interestingly, the last concert he promoted was Russ Taff's final performance with The Imperials at Baylor University. Only divine intervention could orchestrate such a fateful crossroads.

The connection that paved the way for Paul's entry into the group was his friendship with The Imperials' drummer, Tom Reeves. Tom, convinced that Paul would be a perfect fit, handed one of Paul's cassettes to the group, and they were instantly impressed by his vocal prowess. An audition in Nashville soon followed, and within a week, Paul found himself on tour as the newest member of The Imperials.

Paul's addition to the group proved to be the only step that could have continued The Imperials' string of success, not only because of his exceptional singing abilities but also because of his songwriting talents. Even after he departed from The Imperials in 1985, the group continued showcasing his work, including the chart-topping single "Wings of Love" from their album *This Year's Model*, which was co-written by Paul and Keith Thomas.

Interestingly, Paul's journey to The Imperials was not a premeditated pursuit. His initial plan was to focus on solo ministry, but when the opportunity to join the renowned group presented itself, he seized it without hesitation. The group's challenges stemmed from Russ Taff's unprecedented success and the perception that it would be difficult if not impossible for anyone else to fill those shoes. Armond Morales advised Paul, "You've got to cover the songs Russ did, but don't try to be Russ. Just come in and be you." As Paul heeded this advice, his unique vocal abilities soon became a defining aspect of the group's sound. Lonnie Ott, who later sang with Paul in The Imperials, praised Paul's "unique" vocal range, describing it as spanning "from Sting to a true tenor." The current Imperial, Rod Fletcher, echoed similar sentiments, calling Paul "One of the best writers and musicians I've worked with in this genre."

Beyond his musical contributions, Paul also left a lasting impact through his faith and compassion. During an Italian cruise where The Imperials performed before the release of Paul's first album with the group, he had the opportunity to share the gospel with a crew member who had never owned a Bible. Paul provided one and guided the crewman through specific verses, leading the man to accept Christ at an altar call after one of the concerts. The crew member, deeply touched by Paul's kindness, gifted him a shirt from his uniform, which Paul proudly wore on the cover of the album *Stand by the Power*. This album also showcased Paul's songwriting prowess, with him co-writing five out of the ten tracks.

Paul Smith's tenure with The Imperials was a testament to his multifaceted talents and unwavering commitment to his faith. His impact on the group and the lives he touched through his music and ministry continue to resonate, leaving an indelible mark on the Christian music landscape.

The Imperials' 1982 album *Stand by the Power* was a massive success, with multiple chart-topping hits that resonated deeply with fans and industry insiders alike. One song that particularly struck a chord was "Because of Who You Are," which Christian music producer Neal Joseph found especially moving. The album also left a lasting impression on future Imperial Barry Weeks, who named it one of his all-time favorites from the legendary group. Weeks was particularly impressed by the exceptional work of producer Bill Schnee and the talented instrumentalists featured on the record, some of whom were part of the renowned secular rock band Toto.

Among the all-star lineup assembled by Schnee were Toto's legendary drummer Jeff Porcaro and guitarist Steve Lukather, both of whom lent their considerable talents to the album. Schnee highly praised Porcaro, stating, "He would be on every drummer's list of top three drummers." The producer assembled an extraordinary roster of session players, including keyboardist James Newton Howard, whom he described as "one of the top film composers in the business." Bassist Nathan East, who would later join Toto, also played on the album, having previously worked with icons like Stevie Wonder, Sting, and Michael Jackson. Carlos Vega shared drumming duties with Porcaro, and like many others on the record, had an extensive resume working with secular artists and Christian musician Leslie Phillips. Guitarist Hadley Hockensmith rounded out the lineup as a Christian jazz group Koinonia member.

When asked if he felt intimidated by the prospect of producing an Imperials album after Michael Omartian's acclaimed work with the group, Schnee admitted that while he and Omartian were good friends, he was "well aware of what he had done there." Nevertheless, armed with his impressive roster of instrumentalists and the vocal talents of The Imperials, Schnee produced a remarkable album that lived up to its predecessors.

Reflecting on the standout tracks from *Stand by the Power*, Schnee struggled to single out just one, ultimately highlighting three: the title track, "Somebody New," and the ballad "Lord of the Harvest." More than four decades later, Schnee remembered Dave Will's dedication, recalling, "He was sold out. He believed in the ministry. He rebuilt the bus, and I don't think he got paid. He did it for the love of what he was doing."

Speaking of The Imperials' bus, Tim Holder heard a story that will be recounted cryptically to protect the identities involved. It's well-documented that Dave Will bore a striking resemblance to country music star Kenny Rogers. At one point, The Imperials had two buses – one for the singers and one for the band – with a rotating team of drivers comprising singers, band members, and others. One particular driver had a habit of parking in unconventional spaces, leading to occasional confrontations with store owners or managers.

The conversation would typically go like this:

Store Owner/Manager: You can't park there.

Driver: Oh really? Do you know who's on that bus?

Owner/Manager: No.

Driver: Kenny Rogers.

This would usually put an end to the protests. After completing his errand, the driver would approach Dave Will on the singers' bus and say, "Hey, Dave, some guys here want to say hi to you." Dave would warmly greet the individuals, ever the gracious gentleman, leaving them convinced they had met the legendary Kenny Rogers himself. It's hard to say how many people in the early 1980s were duped into thinking they had shaken hands with the country music icon when, in fact, they had encountered David Will of The Imperials.

Talking about life on the bus, Jimmie Lee Sloas, who played for the group in the early 1980s, carved out quite a name for himself with his bandmates. At that time, he served as their bass player but later joined as a vocalist. Keith Thomas, who co-wrote several songs for The Imperials, had high praise for Jimmie's skills, saying, "Jimmie is easily one of the top five bass players in Nashville. I can't articulate how much I respect him. He has an incredible reputation here." With musicians of such caliber both on stage and behind the scenes, it's no wonder *Stand by the Power* left such an indelible mark on contemporary Christian music.

Keith loved Jimmie's great sense of humor, a trait appreciated by other Christian artists like Lisa Bevill and future Imperial Ron Hemby.

The Imperials were super busy at this point, performing around 150 concerts annually! Their schedule even included week-long revival services at some churches where they provided the music. Dave Will handled most of the preaching duties, while Jim Murray continued to inject some much-needed humor into the proceedings.

Around this time, The Imperials did something innovative again. Armond Morales invited his sisters, Pam and Alice, and also Mel Tunney to provide backup vocals on several tour dates. Years later, Mel joined First Call, and Pam became an Imperial herself, proving once more that Armond had an excellent eye for spotting talent.

The awards kept pouring in during this era, too. The Imperials won Dove Awards from 1982 through 1984 for "Male Group of the Year," "Group of the Year," and "Pop/Contemporary Album of the Year." They were on a roll!

Their album *Side by Side* was unique - a double album where each member sang five solo tracks. Neal Joseph produced the songs featuring Jim and Armond on lead vocals, while he split production duties with Keith Thomas for David Will's tracks. Keith solely produced Paul Smith's songs. The rest of The Imperials provided backup vocals on each other's solo cuts.

Neal Joseph revealed that the *Side by Side* concept came from the group members themselves. He said, "They thought showing their personalities and styles would be interesting." Mel Tunney considered it "a brilliant idea" for showcasing the individual talents of the four singers.

A couple of songs Neal produced stood out to him. He loved Jim Murray's ballad "Even the Praise Comes from You," even though the single released was "Sound His Praise." Another noteworthy Jim Murray cut was "Built to Last." It was the first song ever recorded by a young songwriter named Steven Curtis Chapman!

Steven signed with Sparrow Records a few years later and had a spectacular career with 50 number-one hits in Christian music. But getting that first song on an Imperials album was huge for the college kid back then. He shared, "I lost my mind. It couldn't have been a bigger deal." As an

Imperials fan who grew up loving their music, especially the Michael Omartian-produced albums, Steven said, "The Imperials' music blew my mind. Landing "Built to Last" on *Side by Side* was a dream."

Neal's favorite Dave Will song on the album was the worshipful "You're the Only Jesus." As for Paul Smith's section, there were multiple standouts like the fun, upbeat "Here on the Rock" and the delicate ballad "Make My Heart Your Home," a duet with Leslie Phillips, who had a successful string of albums before transitioning to the secular market. Keith Thomas' favorite Paul Smith cut was "Wait upon the Lord," which he said, "sounded like Al Jarreau."

Bonnie Keen of First Call considered Paul "a nice man full of integrity—a very gifted vocalist." Keith summed it up by stating, "Paul Smith is a beast." This is high praise indeed for the incredible talents in this era of The Imperials' storied career.

Paul's songwriting prowess truly shone on the *Side by Side* album. He co-wrote all five tracks where he took the lead vocals and even contributed to two of Dave's songs. Paul also teamed up with Dick Tunney to pen a tune for Armond called "Good Shepherd." Dick had been touring as the keyboardist for The Imperials, and Neal brought him in to play keys on Jim's songs for the *Side by Side* sessions. Dick's wife Mel pointed out that it was pretty unconventional back then for a touring musician to get studio work like that.

Dick was deeply impressed by Armond's remarkable ability to hold his own as a lead vocalist, "not many basses can be (lead) vocalists." It was a testament to Armond's versatility and vocal ability.

In 1984, The Imperials had the honor of performing the title track for a prestigious, various artists' praise album released by their label. *The Praise in Us* compilation featured an impressive lineup of acts, including Kathy Troccoli, David Meece, and interestingly, Russ Taff, who contributed the powerful "Simple Song for a Mighty God." The project's esteemed producer, Neal Joseph, developed the concept and hand-picked the artists, including former Imperial Russ Taff, showcasing his keen eye for talent.

Tom Hemby, who had played guitar in The Imperials' touring band for about five years, decided to pursue other opportunities in 1984, joining Amy Grant's touring band. However, this transition was amicable, as Tom continued collaborating with the group on studio work and songwriting. Armond's open-door policy towards great talent ensured that the relationship remained strong.

1984 also saw the release of *The Imperials Sing the Classics*, which might have left some unfamiliar listeners wondering what the "Classics" referred to. Were they tackling classical hymns? Had contemporary Christian music existed long enough to be considered "classic?" The answer to the latter question was a resounding yes. The album featured ten hit songs from the 1970s and early 1980s written by giants like Bill and Gloria Gaither, Andrae Crouch, Michael Card, Dallas Holm, David Meece, Stormie Omartian, and more. Tracks included beloved hits like "We Are the Reason," "El-Shaddai," "Rise Again," "Because He Lives," and others, solidifying their status as contemporary Christian classics.

Unlike many other albums emphasizing solo vocals, *The Imperials Sing the Classics* leaned heavily into lush four-part harmonies, with any solos being relatively short sections. However, a few singers did get a chance to shine, including the rarity of Armond taking solo leads on back-to-back songs, "We Shall Behold Him" and "Because He Lives," showcasing his versatility once again.

According to the extremely busy producer Neal Joseph, the idea for the classics album came from someone at the record label. The thought was that maybe they could latch onto their previous audiences, since their last albums had been so contemporary/pop. It was a strategic move to appeal to their existing fan base and potentially attract new listeners.

*The Imperials Sing the Classics* ended up being their final release on DaySpring Records, but it was not without fanfare. Interestingly, while they hired a 50-piece orchestra and did one sold-out promotional concert for the album, no actual tour supported it, leaving fans yearning for more live performances of these beloved classics

By this point, having worked extensively with The Imperials, Neal had well-formed opinions of each member and spoke highly of their professionalism and character. "All were great Christian guys who loved the Lord. They never let their success go to their heads. They were very professional and relational. They were not prima donnas at all." It was clear that Neal held The Imperials in high esteem as musicians and individuals.

Regarding Dave Will, Neal said, "I liked the uniqueness of his voice. He had a sweet spirit, and he was funny. His look and style were like Kenny Rogers." Neal appreciated Dave's distinct vocal quality and warm, humorous personality.

The producer also enjoyed collaborating with the group's tenor. "Jim Murray was the consummate professional, always prepared. He worked on songs on his own. He was the quintessential tenor and just a great guy," he said admiringly.

Neal also appreciated what *Side by Side* allowed Armond Morales to showcase. "It gave him a chance to show his versatility. He was a stylized singer. And he was solid as a rock," Neal remarked fondly.

According to Neal, "Paul Smith was a prolific, talented songwriter. He brought a contemporary vibe to the group. His voice was an incredible instrument—it had great dynamics."

Keith Thomas, who worked with The Imperials throughout this period, said admiringly, "All the guys were gifted. I had such respect for all of them. Everybody's contribution made them great."

Keith was an important figure to The Imperials. Bonnie Keen knew him well from the albums he would later produce for First Call. She also sang background vocals on multiple albums he produced for other artists. Bonnie spoke glowingly, "He was a joy in the studio. I learned so much from him as a vocalist. He was a brilliant writer who pushed us without abusing us." The Imperials were blessed with many great musicians, songwriters, and producers like Keith throughout their history.

As interviews were conducted for this book, one last amusing story surfaced regarding this era. Neil Joseph, Keith Thomas, and The Imperials' bass player, Jimmie Lee Sloas, lived on the same street. These three and a fourth neighbor, Dennis Worley, decided to purchase and share a lawnmower jointly. They agreed that the last guy to move out of the neighborhood got to keep the mower. While this anecdote holds no ministry nor musical significance and is only tangentially related to The Imperials, it's a quirky and funny, so we decided to share it here.

After putting out *The Imperials Sing the Classics*, some fans may have wondered if the group was going through an identity crisis. Were they getting reticent about making pop music? The following several albums provided an emphatic answer, starting with *Let the Wind Blow*.

After leaving DaySpring, The Imperials switched to Myrrh Records and were reunited with Brown Banister as their producer. Brown had been a part of their great run in the 1970s.

*Let the Wind Blow* fits in musically with *Priority* and *Stand by the Power*. Paul once again co-wrote five of the album's ten songs. On two songs, "Jericho" and "Not to Us, O Lord," Paul shared the writing credits with Michael W. Smith. Michael also played keyboards on those two pieces. Mike Hudson wrote with the two Smiths on "Jericho." Paul

Smith, Mike Hudson, and Keith Thomas wrote the album's ninth cut, "Miracles," together.

The involvement of Mike Hudson and Brown Banister is significant in The Imperials' history because that duo wrote a couple of songs back on *Heed the Call*. They worked together on "My Mind Forgets a Million Things," which featured a rare Armond solo, and The Imperials' mega hit "Praise the Lord."

It was an exciting time for Christian music in the late 80s. Chris Hauser, who worked in Christian radio back then, recalled that the record label said The Imperials' album *Let the Wind Blow* would have a sound reminiscent of the iconic pop group The Police. Interestingly, this foreshadowed how Paul Smith's second solo album, *No Frills*, after leaving The Imperials, would bear similarities to Sting's music from The Police.

*Let the Wind Blow* was a massive hit, with the title track holding the #1 spot on the charts for an impressive nine weeks. Despite his integral role on that project, Paul didn't stick around for the whole tour cycle. He departed to reignite his blossoming solo career that had been put on hold when he joined the legendary Imperials lineup.

Andy Chrisman of 4Him feels this era of The Imperials is sometimes overlooked, not due to any lack of quality, but because of the immense success of the lineups immediately before and after. He praised Paul as "such a great singer and songwriter."

Paul's first solo release, *Live and Learn*, was a resounding success. Andy hailed it as "one of the greatest albums of all time." Keith Thomas produced it, and Neal Joseph executive produced it. Keith fondly recounted their collaborative experience, noting their shared musical vision and smooth creative process.

For Tim Holder, though, Paul's next album, *No Frills*, was the standout favorite. He reminisced about repeatedly listening to that cassette tape when his CD player was broken. The upbeat tracks and beautiful ballads never grew stale.

Neal Joseph echoed Tim's sentiments, exclaiming, *No Frills* was "one of my all-time favorite albums we did at DaySpring." Keith, who co-produced it with former Imperial Tom Hemby, felt it surpassed the excellence of *Live and Learn*.

When asked for his favorites, Paul cited his next two releases, *Back to Who I Am* and *Human Touch*, as the albums he liked best from his discography. There was certainly no shortage of quality music, though Paul lamented that distribution hurdles limited *Human Touch*'s reach.

After a few more album releases and a stint with Integrity Music as a songwriter, Paul would eventually return to The Imperials. But during his prolific solo stretch, The Imperials faced the difficult task of replacing such a talented singer, respected bandmate, and tireless worker.

**And The Imperials just kept singing...**

## Chapter 9

## Now How Do We Top that?

## 1985-1986

### Armond Morales, Jim Murray, David Will, Danny Ward

After releasing four albums in four years, Paul Smith decided to rededicate himself to his solo career, leaving The Imperials in search of a new lead singer. This opened an exciting opportunity for the legendary group to explore fresh talent and perspectives.

In 1985, an intriguing candidate emerged—Danny Ward. When Keith Thomas first encountered Danny, he was immediately struck by the young man's exceptional vocal abilities. However, Danny's background differed from that of the typical American Christian singer. He hadn't become a believer until age 22 in 1978 and had only been singing professionally since age 18.

Yet, Danny's voice possessed an undeniable quality that captivated audiences. Before The Imperials, he had been the lead singer of Hosanna, a touring group based in Illinois that performed all over the Midwest and Texas. Inspired by Russ Taff's powerful vocals with The Imperials in the late 1970s, Danny had consciously developed a similar sound and style.

Interestingly, when Russ left the group, Danny had received a call from Armond Morales in 1981, inviting him to audition as the new lead singer. While the audition went well, Danny may have sounded too much like a Russ Taff impersonator at the time. Four years later, when Paul Smith departed, the stars aligned, and Danny seized the opportunity to become the new Imperials lead singer.

Danny was determined not to take his time with the legendary group for granted. He marveled at seemingly small moments, like sitting in a hotel room with Jim Murray, an old Elvis concert playing on TV, and realizing that Jim had performed on stage with Elvis during that very concert. But it was about much more than being momentarily starstruck by the history and legacy of The Imperials. As Danny said, "It was a blessing in my life to perform songs like 'Praise the Lord,' 'I'm Forgiven,' and 'Let the Wind Blow' and see God moving in people's lives through the music."

By the end of 1985, Jim Murray decided it was his time to depart the group, seeking a more traditional sound than the edgy, youthful pop direction the new Imperials lineup was taking. Jim went solo for a while, then joined the prestigious Gaither Vocal Band from 1988 to 1992. He has continued to make music since then, occasionally rejoining The Imperials for guest appearances and reunions.

New Year's Day 1986 marked the start of a new calendar year for Ron Hemby and the beginning of his career with the legendary Christian music group, The Imperials - a tenure that would last until August 1990. Before joining The Imperials, Ron had spent around a year and a half touring as a backup singer for Russ Taff. Once he became an Imperial, Ron eventually covered Russ Taff's parts during concerts and on a medley of old hits included on the album *Love's Still Changing Hearts*. However, this was not the role Ron initially envisioned in the group. Late in 1985, during the *Medals* tour, Russ approached Ron and mentioned that Jim Murray was leaving The Imperials. Russ offered to put Ron's name forward to Armond Morales if he was interested.

Ron had been familiar with The Imperials since their early days with Sherman Andrus and Terry Blackwood. He had followed their music through the Andrus and Blackwood Era, and beyond. Naturally, Ron said yes to Russ's offer, though he figured he would need to follow up at some point.

But then a serendipitous event occurred - the buses for Russ Taff's and The Imperials' tours arrived at the same parking lot in Nashville at the same time. Russ took this opportunity to introduce Ron to The Imperials, setting the ball rolling for Ron to join the group.

Eventually, Ron went to Armond Morales's house for an audition, attended by Dave Will and Danny Ward. When Ron said he couldn't be Jim Murray, Armond reassured him, "We don't want you to be Jim Murray. We want you to be Ron Hemby." With that vote of confidence, Ron embraced his unique role and contributed his talents to the ever-evolving legacy of The Imperials.

Many recognized Ron's incredible vocal talent. Andy Chrisman of 4Him described Ron as having "one of the greatest voices in Christian music." Lonnie Ott credited him with a "unique voice" and "an incredible reputation throughout Nashville." Jeoffrey Benward, who had Ron sing backup on one of his albums, said, "Ron is one of the great singers. He had a very distinctive, raw, unusual, soulful voice."

Lisa Bevill, who had sung backup with Ron for Russ Taff, was fascinated by Ron's voice. She recalled that when he warmed up, "He could produce three notes at a time, and it sounded like a train." Witnessing Ron's incredible vocal abilities firsthand was truly an awe-inspiring experience.

James Hollihan wasn't surprised that Ron transitioned from being Russ's backup singer to becoming a full member of The Imperials - Ron's talent was undeniable. James also noted that Ron's exceptional bass playing skills would bring a new dynamic to the quartet's sound.

Legendary producer Keith Thomas, who had previously called Paul Smith a "beast," used the same term for Ron, adding, "He is one of the most amazing singers I have ever worked with. He's got something in his voice and his soul." This is high praise indeed from someone of Keith's caliber and experience in the industry.

A few months after Ron joined the group, Danny Ward left as work began on the album *This Year's Model*. When Danny arrived, Jim Murray saw him as the most well-received member of that particular Imperials lineup. Some felt the quartet was poised to reach the same incredible heights of success they had achieved in their heyday of the late 1970s. However, the record label had different plans, ultimately leading to Danny's departure from the group.

After leaving The Imperials, Danny found himself at a crossroads regarding his vision for music and ministry. He considered staying in the Christian music industry for a time but ultimately decided to pursue church work instead. In 2024, he celebrated an impressive thirty-year tenure at Second Baptist Church in Marion, Illinois—a remarkable achievement by any measure.

Danny's exit paved the way for the return of one of the most dynamic, electrifying musicians ever to be part of The Imperials' storied team, Jimmie Lee Sloas. A new era was about to begin, filled with anticipation and excitement.

**And The Imperials just kept on singing...**

## Chapter 10

## The Incomparable Ron Hemby

## 1986-1989

## Armond Morales, David Will, Ron Hemby, Jimmie Lee Sloas

*This Year's Model* (1987)
*Free the Fire* (1988)

Ron Hemby's addition to The Imperials was a game-changer for the legendary gospel group. Many fans and critics considered him the best lead singer the group ever had, ushering in a new era of supercharged sound and fulfillment of their divine calling.

One of Ron's first moves was to suggest that Armond Morales consider Jimmie Lee Sloas as Danny Ward's replacement. While Jimmie had previously played bass for The Imperials from 1982 to 1984, they had no idea what a talented vocalist he was until he submitted a demo tape of himself singing and playing all the parts for the song "Get Ready." That tape landed Jimmie the job and earned the song a spot on his debut album with the group.

It was a dream come true for Jimmie, having grown up listening to The Imperials. Ron felt Jimmie's creativity impacted the group immensely, and he was right. The three vocalists - Jimmie, Ron, and David Will - would often switch parts fluidly as they made music together over the next few years, with Jimmie handling many leads and Dave taking occasional solos.

Larry Hall, who had worked with The Imperials, raved about Jimmie's incredible talents, calling him "one of the funniest people I've been around" and lauding his freakish abilities as "one of the best bass players I've ever heard, an amazing singer, and an amazing piano player. He's a musical genius."

The group maintained a rigorous touring schedule to support their albums, which Ron admitted was challenging with late nights followed by early morning radio interviews. But it was all worth it for him to make music and do ministry.

When their album *This Year's Model* was released, it was clear this would be a departure from their traditional sound. The cover art sported a quirky 1950s sci-fi theme with stars, a spinning space station, a floating vintage car, and teenagers in 3D glasses - quite a contrast for a group that started in 1963. The music followed suit, with the opening track "Holding On (First Love)" channeling 1950s rock and roll vibes, while "Outlander" may have reminded listeners of the 1981 sci-fi film *Outland* starring Sean Connery.

Music veteran Chris Hauser summed it up best, calling "*This Year's Model* the coolest record they had done." It was The Imperials as you'd never heard them before, and the beginning of an exciting new chapter.

Dan Ames had been a dedicated fan of the iconic group since the late 1960s. When the lineup changed with new members Jimmie Lee Sloas and Ron Hemby joining, he admitted, "It took some getting used to after Russ and Paul. The sound and the look were so different that some of us wondered if they were trying to make it in the secular world. Was the message going to change? Once we calmed down, we saw that it didn't change."

Despite the fresh faces and updated style, fans like Dan could still count on the familiar presence of longtime members Armond Morales and Dave Will in concert. Dan appreciated Dave's unwavering faith, saying, "I loved his heart for the Lord." That devotion shone through when Dan witnessed the group perform during this transitional era.

Fan Tim Holder recalls his initial skepticism upon receiving the group's album *This Year's Model* through a mail-order CD club. "I was so mad when I got that CD. I only received it because it was an automatic shipment that I wanted to cancel, but I forgot. I didn't want to give it a chance. I figured Russ and Paul were great, but what were the odds that the group could catch lightning in a bottle again? I liked Jim's voice too, but he had left after being with them for many years, so I figured he knew something had changed."

However, Tim's reservations melted away as soon as he listened. "The first song blew me away. Usually, I have to listen to an album multiple times before I get into it, but not with *This Year's Model*. Jimmie Lee's high parts and Ron's muscular tenor/baritone, coupled with the brilliance of producer Brown Banister and the established talents of David and Armond, created a great product."

Tim particularly loved the opening track "Holding On" and the soaring vocals on "How Do I Get You?" saying, "The instrumentation at the very end—what Brown Banister did there was like nothing I had heard before. Both of those songs were—and are—amazing."

A noticeable shift occurred in how lead vocals were distributed compared to the previous album, *Let the Wind Blow*. Tim observed, "On *Let the Wind Blow*, David, Jim, and Paul had multiple opportunities to shine. On *This Year's Model*, lead vocals were handled exclusively by the two new guys."

Jimmie Lee took more prominent lead parts in the album's first half, while Ron Hemby's powerful voice drove the latter portion. In fact, Ron ended up with an even bigger role than originally planned when David reassigned the lead for the song "Outlander" to him.

For Ron, the dramatic transition from being the group's tenor to their commanding lead singer and lead soloist was immense. But through it all, Ron Hemby confidently made his mark, solidifying his place in the group's iconic history and future.

It was a grueling process to create that album. Brown Banister's unconventional producing style worked for him, but it pushed the vocalists to their limits. Ron recalls one particular session where they started at 6:00 one evening and didn't wrap up until 5:30 the following morning.

Despite the intense demands, the results spoke for themselves. Andy Chrisman considers *This Year's Model* "the greatest Christian record of all time." He singled out the song "Fallin'" as being especially extraordinary. One of those marathon overnight sessions years earlier had yielded the classic "Praise the Lord," proving Brown's methods could lead to magic.

The new album resonated strongly with younger audiences. Five of the nine tracks hit the Top Ten in 1987, with another peaking at #14. However, for some longtime Imperial fans, *This Year's Model* may have leaned too heavily into a power pop/rock sound. As a result, the group dialed it back slightly on their next release.

Around this era, The Imperials did something unexpected for a veteran act - they worked with a concert performance specialist named Tom Jackson. Jackson is an expert who has coached countless major artists like Taylor Swift, LeCrae, Francesca Battistelli, and Phillips, Craig, and Dean over the years. Surprisingly, The Imperials enlisted his guidance despite Armond Morales having been in the group for over two decades and David Will being there for more than ten years. But it demonstrated Armond's commitment to continually improving and pushing the group forward.

Between *This Year's Model* and their next album, *Free the Fire*, The Imperials lost a key non-singing member when longtime drummer Tom Reeves decided to leave touring life behind in 1988 after nine years on the road with them.

Tom went on to produce and record thousands of musical works. Beyond the prominent lead vocalists, one critical but often overlooked element of The Imperials' success was the talented collaborators who helped craft some of their best music. These unsung heroes burned the midnight oil at truck stops, brainstorming ways to elevate the live experience. Dedicated band members like Tom strived to deliver studio-quality performances while upholding the legendary standard that The Imperials had set across multiple decades. This is where the real work got done.

During his nine-year tenure as The Imperials' drummer and eventual band director, Tom played over 1,500 shows with them. Like many other stellar musicians who backed the group, Tom wasn't looking for accolades. However, any examination of the history of this famous CCM quartet must acknowledge the hard work and exceptional talent of those who provided the rock-solid musical foundation and unwavering commitment to the group's mission.

Tom's story with The Imperials didn't end there, however. He returned years later to produce their 2023 album *Blessed*.

Back in 1988, *Free the Fire* arrived. While perhaps more restrained than its predecessor, it remained a pop-oriented album blending upbeat numbers with ballads. It also featured a couple of abbreviated "I Just Came to Praise the Lord" renditions, tipping the hat to The Imperials' history by opening with the original version before the new guys took over with short solo spots for Ron and Jimmie. This tribute cut had previously appeared on *No Shortage*, exemplifying how The Imperials have excelled at honoring nostalgia while still sounding fresh and modern.

Sadly, *Free the Fire* ended this lineup as Jimmie Lee Sloas departed after the album. In addition to his vocal and songwriting contributions, Jimmie alternated bass guitar duties with Ron during his Imperials tenure. Years later, he would look back and reflect, "The Imperials...was an amazing thing to be a part of." Jimmie Lee Sloas is better known today for his producing and instrumental work.

Fortunately for Imperials fans, he took himself seriously enough as a singer to help create two excellent albums with the group.

It was tough for Ron Hemby when Jimmie left The Imperials because they had worked so well together. Both professionally, making great music, and personally, laughing a lot while doing it, they were close friends and collaborators. Thankfully, Jimmie Lee played an active role in contemporary Christian and country music for many more years after leaving The Imperials. His first job as a studio musician was on the Brown Banister-produced song "Say Once More," which Amy Grant recorded for her *Lead Me On album* in 1988. Throughout the 1990s, Jimmie was the producer for the Christian group Pray For Rain, later called "PFR."

Later, he did a couple of albums as part of a duo called Dogs of Peace. These albums own a piece of music history. Their first album, *Speak*, was released in 1996. Their second, *Heel*, came out in 2016 - a whopping twenty years later. The twenty-year span between the group's first and second releases is a wider gap than any other first and second release in music history, an incredible feat.

The cover art on *Heel* is pretty special and symbolic. The first album featured two well-dressed dogs, which was a fairly on-the-nose reference to a two-man band with "Dogs" in their name. And "Speak" and "Heel" fit the theme as typical dog commands. But then the cover art for the second album gets particularly interesting - *Heel* depicts a sneakered heel with a snake wrapped around the ankle and underfoot. It's a nice reference to Genesis Chapter Three and the prophecy of Jesus, the Seed of Eve, crushing the serpent's head.

Jimmie also co-produced music for singer and Hollywood actor Christian Kane, who starred on the TV shows *Leverage* and *The Librarians*. Some other major artists that Jimmie Lee produced or played for over his prolific career include Garth Brooks, Reba McEntire, Carman, Keith Urban, and Switchfoot. Surprisingly, he even worked with the heavy metal group Megadeth at one point!

Lisa Bevill, a Christian singer, enjoyed working with Jimmie when he produced her *Love of Heaven* album in the 2000s. She remembered him as "really gifted, very humble," and one of the funniest people she has known behind the scenes.

The Imperials felt the loss of Jimmie Lee Sloas when he departed the group after helping make them a significant act in the 1970s. However, his musical legacy and impact stretched far beyond those two albums with Ron Hemby and The Imperials.

**And The Imperials just kept singing...**

# Chapter 11

## The Imperials Return to a familiar Sound

## 1989-1990

## Armond Morales, David Will, Ron Hemby, David Robertson, Jason Beddoe

### *Love's Still Changing Hearts* (1990)

*Love's Still Changing Hearts* was a significant album for The Imperials in 1990. With Jimmie Lee Sloas's departure, Pennsylvania native David Robertson joined the group, sharing lead and tenor vocals with Ron Hemby. David had an interesting backstory - he was a preacher's kid who initially pursued a secular music career in Los Angeles. However, as he shared in his first solo album's liner notes, he started "drifting away from all [he'd] been taught to embrace." Thankfully, two friends invited him to a Bible study led by Pat Benatar's mother, Millie Andrzejewski, which proved pivotal. David reflected, "Little did I know that this would be the night God would change my life. Thank God for servants."

Leaving behind his secular ambitions, David found his way to The Imperials in Tennessee. Michelle Younkman, who worked at Star Song records, remembered him as not only musically gifted but also "introspective" and a diligent worker. Current Imperial Rod Fletcher praised David as "an amazing talent; an amazing singer," a sentiment echoed by Barry Weeks, who called him "one of my top, top favorite singers—an incredible, unique singer."

Though brief, David's tenure left a mark. He wrote and sang lead on the hit "It's Raining Again" and co-wrote "I Will Follow You" and "Come Let Us Worship."

David Will, also contributed in a special way on this album, taking the lead on "Come Let Us Worship" and

75

"Goin' Away" - the latter co-written by Jimmie Lee Sloas, post-departure.

The album had a pop sound with blues influences from Ron Hemby, particularly evident on tracks like "It's Gonna Be Alright," which he wrote and sang lead on. The title track, co-written by Justin Peters and Ron's brother Tom, also had a bluesy vibe. Armond Morales played a bigger role, serving as an executive producer, while his son Jason provided background vocals, foreshadowing his future involvement.

Overall, *Love's Still Changing Hearts* represented an intriguing transition for The Imperials, blending new and old talents to create a distinctive sound that resonated with fans.

The *Loves Still Changing Hearts* album by The Imperials is particularly noteworthy for its extensive medley featuring the group's greatest hits from the Russ Taff era and beyond. It's a nostalgic trip down memory lane for longtime fans.

Speaking of unique collaborations, The Imperials had an intriguing experience as guest vocalists on the title track of the Gaither Vocal Band's 1990 album *A Few Good Men*. The Gaither Vocal Band was known for contemporary Christian music in the '80s, but *A Few Good Men* had more of a southern gospel vibe. However, the title song itself was a typical contemporary ballad.

To add to the genre-blending, The Imperials, who had transitioned to a more contemporary sound, joined the decidedly southern gospel group The Cathedrals on the track, along with Christian rocker Mylon LeFevre. It was an unusual mix, but the final result was still a solid song.

Another interesting Imperial footnote from 1990 involves the various artists' project *Handel's Young Messiah*. The Imperials contributed "O Thou That Tellest," with Ron Hemby on lead vocals. Former Imperial Russ Taff also appeared, duetting with Sheila Walsh on "He Shall Feed His Flock." Interestingly, one of the producers was Paul Mills, who would go on to produce an Imperials album shortly after.

After recording just one album with The Imperials, David Robertson departed to pursue a solo career. He also became involved with Kingdom Building Ministries, an organization focused on discipling young people and adults.

In 1992, Robertson collaborated with Christian artist Kelli Reisen on the excellent duet "You Were Sent for Me" from her *Dream of a Lifetime* album. Surprisingly, the song made it onto the Unforgettable Duets, Vol. 2 compilation despite never being released as a single.

For Reisen, working with Robertson held special significance. As a teenager singing in her church's youth choir, she fondly remembered traveling and singing along to Imperials hits like "Praise the Lord," "Trumpet of Jesus," and "Sail On." She reflected, "When I had a chance to sing with an Imperial, it was crazy. They ministered to me. God used their gifts...It was a full-circle moment. They minister to me to this day."

Star Song executive Darrell A. Harris praised Robertson's immense "heart for the Lord that was always overflowing."

Robertson went on to release three critically acclaimed solo albums in the 1990s with a blue-eyed soul style. His debut *Soul Embrace* featured the poignant "Goodbye to Me," which Reisen called "one of the all-time best songs in Christian music." The song's honest exploration of the tension between serving God and serving self deeply impacted Reisen and others.

Producer Paul Mills, who helmed *Soul Embrace* and Robertson's sophomore effort, *Someone Who Cares*, and The Imperials' *Stir It Up*, fondly remembered Robertson as "a great guy and singer" who was "always smiling and happy" - a wonderful legacy.

Notably, *Soul Embrace* included Robertson's original "What Once Was a River," recently recorded by the Gaither Vocal Band.

After Robertson's departure, Jason Beddoe briefly replaced him in The Imperials' lineup. An accomplished vocalist who had worked with artists like Dolly Parton, Carman, and Kerry Livgren, Beddoe only remained long enough to begin recording the group's next album. His exit prompted leader Armond Morales to take an unprecedented step.

**And The Imperials just kept singing**...

The 1967 Imperials
Back row: Armond Morales, Roger Wiles, Joe Moscheo
Front row: Terry Blackwood, Jim Murray

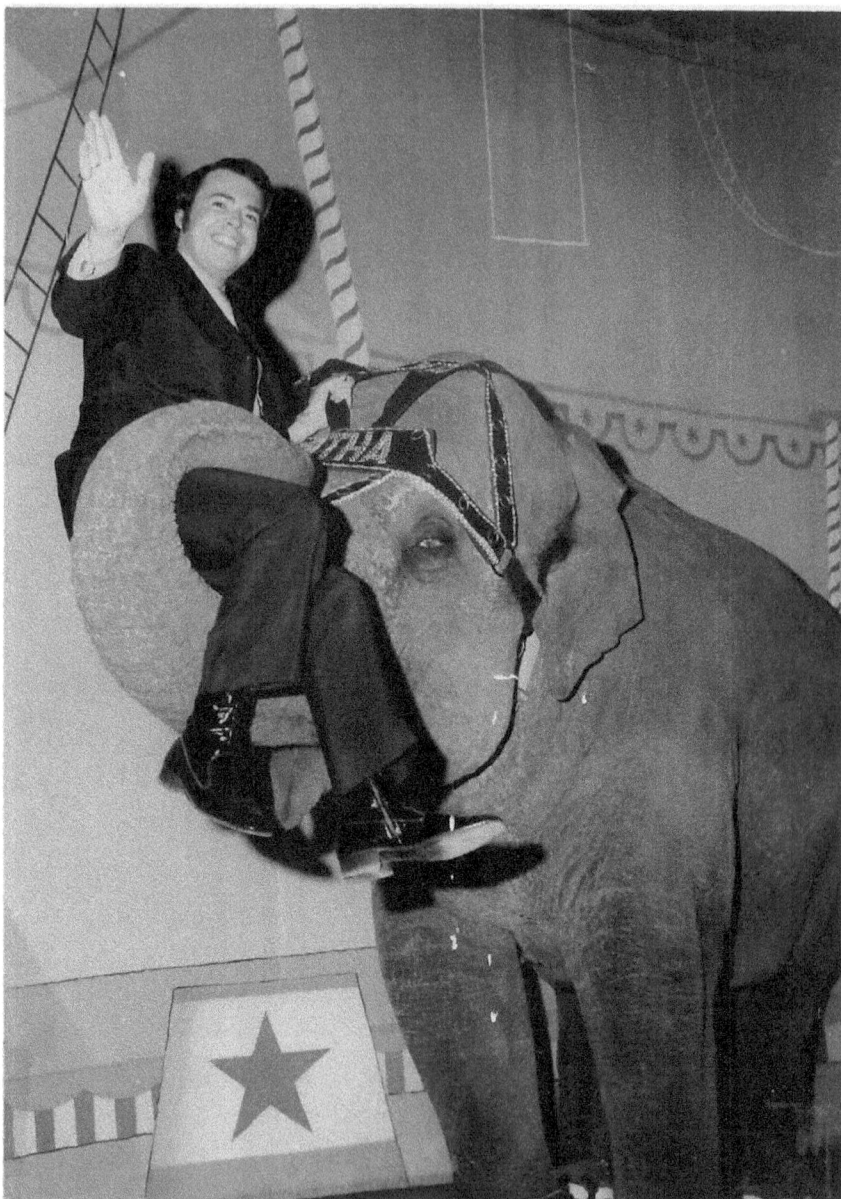

Jim Murray and an elephant
(Because how could we not include this awesome pic?)

The Imperials with Elvis
Back Row: Joe Moscheo, Jim Murray, Elvis Pressley,
Armond Morales, Greg Gordon
Front Row: Terry Blackwood

The Imperials circa 1971
Third Row: Greg Gordon
Second Row: Terry Blackwood, Jim Murray
First Row: Joe Moscheo, Armond Morales

Front Row: The Imperials—Terry Blackwood, Sherman Andrus, Armond Morales, and Jim Murray

Back Row: Solid Rock (The Imperials' road band in that era) Jeff Catren, Mike Padgett, Jeff Chambers, and Chuck Wright

Jim Murray, Terry Blackwood, Sherman Andrus, Armond Morales

Jim Murray, Dave Will, Russ Taff, Armond Morales

Jim Murray, Paul Smith, Dave Will, Armond Morales

Bill Schnee, Armond Morales, Michael Omartian (at the piano),
Jimmie Lee Sloas, Ron Hemby, Dave Will

Dave Will, Dave Robertson, Armond Morales

Steve Ferguson, Jeff Walker, radio host Steve Krampitz,
David Will, Armond Morales

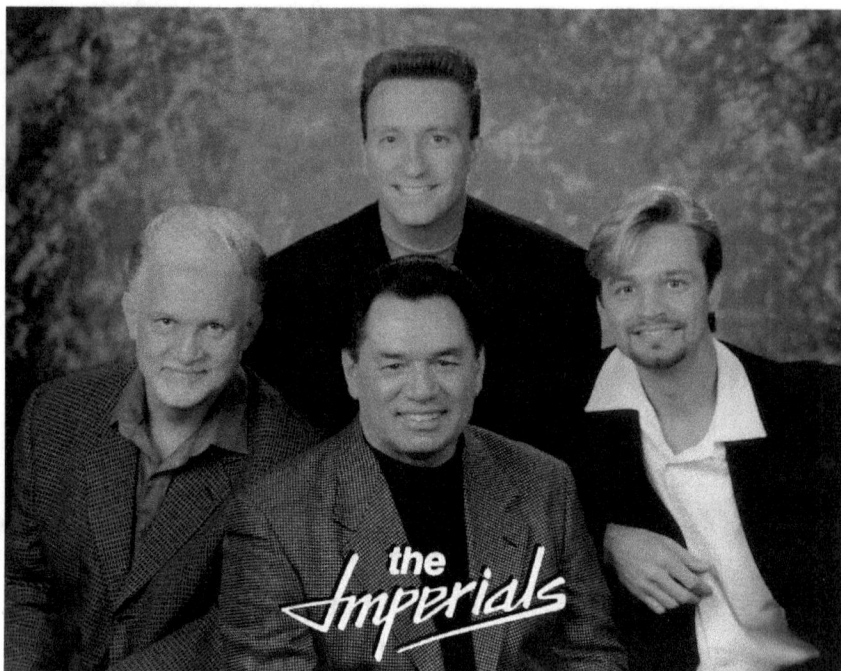

Dave Will, Armond Morales (front row), Barry Weeks
(back row), Steve Ferguson

Jim Murray, Russ Taff, Dave Will, Armond Morales
Back Row: Tim Norris

Dave Will, Rick Evans, Armond Morales, Jim Murray

Armond Morales, Rick Evans, Dave Will, Paul Smith

Michael Schlee, Paul Smith, Russ Taff, Rick Evans, Lonnie Ott

Rod Fletcher, Paul Smith, Ron Hemby, Rick Evans

Rick Evans, Debra Evans, Denise Smith, Paul Smith

Rick Evans

Brenda and Jim Murray

Sherman Andrus

David Will

Armond Morales

## Chapter 12

## Rick Evans Story and a Whole New Direction

## 1990-1993

## Armond Morales, David Will, Ron Hemby, Jason Beddoe, Jonathan (Pierce) Hildreth, Pam Morales

*Big God* (1991)
*Stir It Up* (1992)

When Ron and David left, The Imperials faced a true crossroads. After years of evolution and success, the group wanted to find a more evangelical platform without losing their contemporary Christian music edge and presence.

Enter Rick Evans, a familiar face who had gotten to know Armond Morales, attended their concerts, and even opened for The Imperials in California with his former group. When The Imperials began searching for new members, Rick's name came up, and Armond invited him to audition in Nashville. Convinced this was God's will, Rick went all-in - he bought a 2,500 square foot house on five acres in Franklin, Tennessee before even auditioning!

Rick vividly recalls showing the house to Armond, who phoned his wife Bonnie incredulously saying, "I hope he can sing." The audition went well from Rick's perspective, with David Robertson and David Will offering encouragement. But when Armond emerged, he delivered a disappointing verdict: "I love your voice, but..." Armond felt Rick looked too similar to former member Paul Smith and decided to go another direction.

Though let down, Rick remained faithful to his calling. "Within a few months, the two businesses I owned in California collapsed, I had no job, $90,000 in debt, and a daughter to provide for," he recounted. Yet God provided opportunities to sing at Harvest Crusades with Pastor Chuck

Smith and Greg Laurie, tour with the Dennis Agajanian Band alongside the Billy Graham Evangelistic Association, and perform for Promise Keepers.

Despite the setback, Rick harbored no ill will toward The Imperials. He continued attending their shows, and his friendship with Armond grew. Armond affectionately dubbed him "the fifth Imperial." Rick learned that a deferred dream isn't necessarily denied - he'd need to await the Lord's timing patiently.

Meanwhile, Ron Hemby had enjoyed his time with The Imperials, but after many successes that included singing lead on five #1 hits, he was ready for a slower pace closer to home. Counting his time with The Imperials, Russ Taff and others, he had spent 15 years on the road. Ron's commitment to music and ministry never waned. He joined the country trio Buffalo Club, releasing an album in 1997 before eventually rejoining his old band, The Imperials.

The story of how Jonathan Hildreth joined The Imperials is a fascinating one. As most fans know, he replaced Ron Hemby after Naomi Judd, the country music star, heard Jonathan sing. Naomi and Jonathan attended Christ Church in Nashville, and Jonathan was in the choir there. One Sunday, he performed a solo, and Naomi was impressed by his vocal abilities. On her recommendation, The Imperials decided to take a chance on him.

According to Michelle Younkman, who worked closely with the group during this era, Jonathan's sound was somewhat similar to that of David Robertson, the previous tenor. Both men possessed immense talent and could create a dynamic, blue-eyed soul sound, a hallmark of The Imperials' style.

The group had already started recording their album *Big God* before Jason Beddoe's departure, and Pam Morales, Armond's sister, replaced him. This wasn't Pam's first time with the group, as she had previously sung backup vocals for them on the road in the early 1980s. However, she would now become the first and only woman to be an official member of the iconic quartet.

Some fans initially doubted how Pam's voice might fit in with The Imperials, especially on their older songs, and Pam herself shared those concerns. She worried that she might sound "too girly." But what made her voice truly special was her ability to hit high notes and, in her own words, "sound like a man sometimes." The group was getting the best of both worlds with Pam's unique vocal talents.

Long-time listener Allan Stenmark, who saw The Imperials perform in Finland in the early 1990s, thought Pam's voice blended quite well with the guys. To make it even more of a family affair, Jason Morales, Armond's son, joined the tour crew and ran sound during their concerts.

The first album by this new lineup was *Big God*, produced by the legendary Ken Mansfield. Ken had an extraordinary career, having worked with major artists like the Beatles, Dolly Parton, Judy Garland, David Cassidy, and many more. Interestingly, *Big God* was Ken's first Christian album.

The title track from *Big God* became a huge hit for the group. Each member got a chance to showcase their vocal talents, and Armond had the rare opportunity to be the first voice heard on the song. It was so popular that a later version of The Imperials re-recorded it more than a decade later.

According to Michelle Younkman, The Imperials continued touring extensively during this period. "They were workhorses. They loved their fans and wanted to be out there with them," she said.

Their next album, *Stir It Up*, was amazingly good. Produced by Paul Mills, it had a slick, pop sound that shouldn't have been too surprising, given Paul's successful work with the contemporary Christian music group Phillips, Craig, and Dean. The quality of his first album with that trio had put him on The Imperials' radar. As Paul said, his trio work "opened many doors for me. It was a God thing."

A long-time fan, Barry Weeks considered *Stir It Up* phenomenal and thought Jonathan had an "elite voice."

Interestingly, both *Big God* and *Stir It Up* were executive produced by Armond. The long-time bass singer sat down with Star Song record executive Jeff Moseley and Paul Mills, and the three of them discussed creating an album with a more pop sound than *Big God*. Paul listened to that album to assess where the foursome was vocally and hear who could sing what.

His favorite song on *Big God* was the title track. "I liked the song 'Big God.' That was the first time I studied Armond's big, rich voice. And I loved it," Paul said.

Paul enjoyed the entire record-making process with all four members. "Armond had a lot of trust, which I appreciated. I wanted to do a good job for him. Dave was a super nice guy. Anything I needed, he was willing to try. He was the ultimate gentleman.

The dynamic between Jonathan Pierce and Pam Morales was unique when recording solo tracks for the album *Stir It Up*. Unlike the other members who would typically record alone, Jonathan and Pam showed up during each other's vocal sessions. As Paul Mills, the producer, explained, "They were very supportive of each other. They encouraged each other. The studio can be sterile. You don't have the concert adrenaline." Their mutual presence provided a much-needed energy boost. At times while producing an album, Paul has resorted to standing up and waving his arms to infuse extra liveliness into the recording process. With Pam and Jonathan showing up for each other, Paul did not have to resort to such tactics, which made their sessions more enjoyable for everyone involved.

Looking back, Paul found it impossible to single out a favorite track from *Stir It Up*—the entire album was a gem. However, he did express a particular fondness for songs like

"Taking Your Love for Granted," "Change Your World," and "Stir It Up," all of which featured Jonathan's powerful lead vocals, as well as "We're All Looking," which showcased Pam's incredible talent.

Christian recording artist Lisa Bevill, who lent her vocals as a backup singer on the album, held Paul Mills' work in high regard, not just for this project but for his numerous other contributions to the industry.

As the *Stir It Up* sessions drew to a close, Pam decided to retire from life on the road, following in the footsteps of many Imperials before her. Not long after, Jonathan also announced his departure from the group, intending to pursue a solo career and an opportunity to sing with the renowned Gaither Vocal Band.

Interestingly, Jonathan also dropped his last name, opting to go by "Jonathan Pierce" professionally, since "Pierce" was his middle name. This decision coincided with a distinct shift in his musical style – while his four solo albums embraced a pop/R&B sound, his work with the Gaither Vocal Band (from 1994 to 1997) remained firmly rooted in the southern gospel tradition. It was a remarkable feat. Artists like Russ Taff and Michael English have also successfully navigated both genres throughout their careers, but Jonathan managed to do so simultaneously.

Jonathan's debut solo effort, *One Love*, included a cover of Stevie Wonder's "Heaven Is Ten Zillion Light Years Away" and boasted an impressive lineup of producers. Michael Omartian helmed four tracks, John and Dino Elefante produced three, and Guy Roche oversaw the remaining four.

His follow-up album, *Mission*, continued the trend of enlisting multiple producers. Guy Roche returned, joined by the incomparable Brown Banister. Bob Parr produced one song solo and collaborated with Alex Seidl on others. Notably, this album also featured a reimagined version of the beloved Imperials hit "Praise the Lord," a nod to Jonathan's roots.

For his third solo effort, *Sanctuary*, Jonathan entrusted the production duties entirely to Phil Naish, a seasoned veteran with an impressive track record working with artists like Steven Curtis Chapman, First Call, Geoff Moore, Point of Grace, Michael Card, and, perhaps most relevantly, Russell Taff, whose 2018 album *Believe* was co-produced by Phil and Mark Hornsby.

Jonathan's final solo album, *For You*, was primarily produced by Brian Rawling. One track, "Still the Love of My Life," was co-produced and co-written by the legendary Michael Bolton. Another standout moment was "Let Your Soul Be Your Pilot," penned by Sting.

Despite the diverse array of collaborators and musical influences, Jonathan remained steadfast in his faith, as evidenced by his liner notes which read in part, "And to the Maker of all things and the Giver of the Gift, my Savior Jesus Christ, it is for You."

However, Jonathan's passion for the music industry had waned by 2003, the same year *For You* was released. He traded in his microphone for a career in interior design, accepting a position on the Country Music Television show *Ultimate Country Home*.

For The Imperials, Pam and Jonathan's departures marked yet another crossroads, prompting the group to once again reinvent themselves and head in a new creative direction, as they had done numerous times before.

This was a remarkable period for The Imperials, with new members, new sounds, and continued success. Their ability to evolve and adapt while staying true to their roots is a testament to their continued legacy and their place in CCM royalty.

**And The Imperials just kept singing…**

## Chapter 13

## The Church Years

### 1993

### Armond Morales, David Will, Mark Addock, Brian Comeaux, Peter Pankratz, Bill Morris

The Imperials' journey took an unexpected turn after their acclaimed *Stir It Up* album in 1992. Two pivotal members, Jonathan and Pam, decided to part ways with the group, leaving a void that needed to be filled. Enter Brian Comeaux, who stepped up as the new lead vocalist, but the group's lineup remained in flux as they cycled through three different tenors within a year.

Brian's tenure with The Imperials was short-lived, as he eventually left to pursue pastoral ministry. Fast forward to early 2025, and he's now leading a church in Canada, following his calling to spread the Word.

One of the tenors who graced The Imperials' lineup during that time had a particularly intriguing backstory. Peter Pankratz and his brother Nikolai defected from the former Soviet Union during the tense Cold War Era of the 1980s. They sought refuge in the United States, forming a Christian band called "The Russians." The brothers released two albums under that moniker before rebranding themselves as "Ruscha" for their 1988 release, *Come Alive*. If you're feeling nostalgic, you might still be able to find their power ballad single "Come Home" online, a quintessential 1980s gem.

After their stint with Ruscha, the Siberian brothers went their separate ways. Some of their former bandmates then formed a Christian hard rock group called "Legend," which later became "Legend Seven," which released several albums in the early 1990s.

Amidst all these lineup changes, one constant remained: Bill Morris, a true Renaissance man in Christian entertainment. Morris has graced the stages of CBS, NBC, TBN, and PBS with his multifaceted talents as a singer, writer, director, and producer, leaving an indelible mark on the industry.

**And The Imperials just kept singing…**

## 1994-1996

### Armond Morales, David Will, Steven Ferguson, Jeff Walker

*Treasures* (1994)
*'Til He Comes* (1995)

Armond and Dave found some stability with Steven Ferguson's arrival in 1994. Steve stayed with the group for about five years, and these three recorded multiple albums. Steven sang tenor, and their new lead vocalist in the mid-1990s was Jeff Walker.

It's worth noting that Steve and Jeff were ordained ministers when they joined the group. The Imperials had prioritized ministry in their work for quite some time, and with the addition of Steve and Jeff, they leaned further in this direction, performing more in churches and less in concert venues.

You might think that most Christian artists have the same basic mindset: make music for the glory of God. But the reality is that musicians in this industry have different agendas. Take Lisa Bevill, for instance. She released five Christian albums and sang backup on countless others. Lisa was very adamant about making music for the Lord.

"Early in my career, when I was a backup singer on the road, there were some big concerts in arenas, and the CCM artist I traveled with never offered an altar call," she said. "There was never coordination with local pastors or any outreach to support them. I saw these massive captive audiences, but an opportunity was lost."

Lisa recognized that she wanted to do things differently when performing her music on the road. "When I was an artist, I felt it was a calling. It was far more about ministry than music. Music was the tool to get me to true ministry. I wanted to make music for hurting people who needed Jesus."

She continued, "If you don't have God in it, what's the point? It should be a calling. My favorite part of doing concerts was talking to people afterwards. It's a heavy weight to be called by God to be an artist. It's so much bigger than music. The real work to me is ministry."

Steven Curtis Chapman felt the same way. He decided early on to pursue a career in Christian music instead of country music or anything else. "Christian music was so important to me because the songs I was listening to discipled me," he said. "That was what drew me to The Imperials. They were doing great music and pushing the envelope, but at the heart of it, I was being discipled."

So you see, some artists in contemporary Christian music are ministers who use music as a tool, some Christians want to make a living providing wholesome entertainment, and some musicians want to make music. Christian music opened the door for them. The Imperials had long cared about ministry but would take it to a new level in this era.

One of the concert dates that The Imperials did in 1994 was at First Church of the Nazarene in Springfield, Illinois. It was Steve Krampitz's church, and he had the honor of introducing them. According to Steve, their music in 1994 was a little toned down from the Ron Hemby, Jimmie Lee Sloas, and Jonathan Hildreth days and more of a middle of the road style, as they mixed some classic Imperials songs in with new material.

*Treasures* was a "Best Of" album that came out in 1994 and only covered their last three records. It is relatively common for a project like this to have a new song at the beginning or end of the compilation, but The Imperials tucked their new work right in the middle. "I Don't Live There Anymore," the lone original, was the seventh of the thirteen songs. It had an excellent Imperials-caliber pedigree since it was written by Ron and Tom Hemby and produced by Paul Mills. Jeff Walker did an outstanding job singing lead on it.

The release of *'Til He Comes* in 1995 captured the group's middle of the road style. This musical offering was well-suited for the adult contemporary sound many Christian radio stations preferred. One strong exception to that was a legitimately funky tune called "Say So," written by Andrae Crouch.

Ah, The Imperials' album '*Til He Comes* - a true labor of love and a testament to the group's enduring talent and camaraderie. Let's go ahead and dive into the making of this gem.

The members shared the workload with the new guys, Steve and Jeff, getting ample chances to showcase their skills. Dave lent his vocals to the title track, while Armond's presence was more pronounced on this Brian Green-produced album than on many others. The long-time bass singer even had a short solo to kick off the song "We Believe." And as if that wasn't enough, Armond treated us to a full-length solo on the album's closing number, "Standing in the Presence of the King," with the rest of the fellas providing backing vocals. Simply sublime!

Now, while '*Til He Comes* may not have spawned a slew of chart-toppers like some of The Imperials' previous efforts, it did manage to snag one hit. "The Power of Praise," penned by the dynamic duo of Geoff and Becky Thurman, peaked at a respectable #27 on the Adult Contemporary charts.

As expected, Armond took the reins as executive producer, ensuring the album's quality from start to finish.

Tom Hemby, a veteran of The Imperials' touring band, stepped up to the plate and played all the acoustic and electric guitar parts on the album. Talk about a professional leap! Tom's transition from road warrior to studio wizard was a path well-trodden by many Imperials band members, including the likes of Dick Tunney, James Hollihan, and Tom Reeves. A true testament to the strength of that touring ensemble in the 70s and 80s.

And speaking of Tom Hemby, the man's a force to be reckoned with in the music biz. He's worked with legends like Elvis Presley, Amy Grant, Michael W. Smith, BeBe Winans, Steven Curtis Chapman, and countless others. His success can be attributed to two key factors: firstly, his undeniable talent, which has earned him multiple Dove Awards and a GRAMMY, not to mention the respect of the industry's finest. Secondly, his impeccable character. As Tom himself put it, "I've always been one to exercise the Golden Rule. Just treat people simply as you would want to be treated. It always works in every aspect of life. I've just been grateful and humble to be associated with so many great people in the world of ministry and arts through the years!"

And lastly, a quick nod to The Imperials for getting "'Til" right on this album title. It's a common mistake - many people render it "till," but they nailed it! Remember, dear reader, grammar is your friend.

*'Til He Comes* is an album that showcased The Imperials' talent, camaraderie, and commitment to excellence. Here's to many more years of inspiring music from this legendary group!

**And The Imperials just kept singing...**

## 1996-1997

## Armond Morales, David Will, Steven Ferguson, Steve Shapiro

*It's Still the Cross* (1996)
*Legacy* (1996)

After Jeff Walker departed, Steve Shapiro joined the group as the new lead singer in 1996. It was an exciting time for The Imperials, with two new albums hitting the market that year.

The current group released new music on the album "It's Still the Cross." Steve Ferguson, a group member, convinced them to let his friend Barry Weeks produce the album. Barry was a long-time Imperial fan from Roanoke, Virginia, who had been singing and producing local artists in the area. He eagerly accepted the opportunity to work with The Imperials.

Barry's musical influences, such as Manhattan Transfer, Take 6, and NewSong, shaped the layered vocal style he brought to *It's Still the Cross* and the subsequent Christmas album he produced for the group. However, the album also catered to the group's older fans by including a re-recording of the classic "Big God" from earlier in the 1990s and "Same Old Fashioned Way," a song penned by Dave Will. Dave took the lead on this track, which was initially recorded on the unreleased *Lost Album* in 1976 but wasn't officially released until 2006.

Another significant release in 1996 was *Legacy*, a double-disc compilation featuring thirty-four of The Imperials' hit songs from 1977 to 1988. This gave fans a comprehensive collection of their most popular tracks from that era.

Ministry remained a priority for The Imperials during their concerts, and long-time fan Phil Brown experienced a noteworthy blessing during this period. Phil's

110

first date with his future wife had been an Imperials concert during their *Heed the Call* tour in the late 1970s. In 1997, at another Imperials concert, their oldest daughter, aged seven, prayed to receive Christ as her Savior. This blessed moment occurred as she prayed with Armond Morales, a touching experience for the family.

This era also saw some of The Imperials become part of the ongoing Elvis phenomenon. A show called "Elvis: The Concert" was launched, featuring vocalists and instrumentalists who had previously performed with Elvis Presley. Since Elvis had passed away two decades earlier, the show utilized videos of his performances projected on a big screen, with the musicians performing live alongside the footage. The show went on tour in Europe, Asia, and Australia.

Jim Murray, Terry Blackwood, Armond Morales, and Joe Moscheo were involved in the production, having worked with Elvis in the past. Even though Sherman Andrus had not performed with Elvis in concert, he had participated in the all-night singing sessions that Elvis loved, so he was also part of the show, allowing these former Imperials to relive their connection to theirs with Elvis Presley.

**And The Imperials just kept singing…**

## 1997-1999

### Armond Morales, David Will, Steven Ferguson, Barry Weeks

#### *Songs of Christmas* (1998)
#### *Hall of Fame* (1999)

It had been nearly two decades since The Imperials released a Christmas album when they finally broke that drought with *Songs of Christmas* in 1997. This project held a special place in the heart of Barry Weeks, who had taken over as the group's lead singer that fall after Steve Shapiro's departure.

"*Songs of Christmas* was relaxed and fun. There was less stress for the group. It was more timeless. It was my favorite to do—the most natural. I still love that record today," Barry reminisced.

While Barry sang many lead parts during The Imperials' tours, Dave Will was the primary vocalist on the Christmas record, with the other guys chiming in here and there. However, this wasn't a solo-driven album by any means—it featured lush harmonies and layered vocals.

Phil Brown, pleased with Barry's production choices, raved about Dave's emotive vocals. "You could count on Dave Will to take a song and reach into your soul. He had a great voice for that kind of thing." Phil also shared that *Songs of Christmas* has remained one of his yuletide favorites.

For his part, Tim Holder singled out "I Have Seen the Light" and "O Come, O Come, Emmanuel" as standout tracks. "Both songs have tight, clear vocals and smooth instrumentation. This is just an impressively-produced album."

1998 proved a landmark year, as The Imperials were inducted into the Gospel Music Association's Gospel Music Hall of Fame. Ten group members spanning different eras - the five original Imperials, Terry Blackwood, Sherman Andrus, Joe Moscheo, Jim Murray, and Russ Taff - attended the official ceremony.

To commemorate the honor, The Imperials released the *Hall of Fame* album in early 1999, containing 25 of their most popular Blackwood/Andrus Era songs.

At this stage, the group continued touring extensively, hitting the road for over 250 dates per year across 48 states and venturing to Haiti. While they'd perform a medley of classic hits to appease nostalgic fans, Barry estimates that 80% of their set list featured newer material, as Armond Morales was keen on keeping The Imperials innovative.

The concerts continued to blend music with ministry, as Dave Will frequently preached during the shows. "He was a preacher trapped in a singer's body. An Old Testament eschatology student. He only thought about serving God and constantly waiting for Christ to return. He was always talking about God. It was a great example for us," Barry reflected. Thankfully, Dave didn't shoulder the spiritual burden alone, as Barry, Steve Ferguson, and even Armond would also share words between songs, which suited their callings.

After *Songs of Christmas*, Steve Ferguson exited The Imperials, though he'd resurface on some Gaither Homecoming Videos. He has also appeared on television networks worldwide and been involved in charity work. Steve eventually became a pastor in South Dakota for many years.

**And The Imperials just kept singing**…

### 1999-2000

### Armond Morales, David Will, Barry Weeks, Jeremie Hudson, Jason Hallcox, Jason Morales

As the 20th century drew to a close, The Imperials underwent significant changes again. After Steven Ferguson's departure, Jeremie Hudson stepped in as the new tenor. But that transition paled in comparison to what followed in January 2000 – the losses of their lead singer, Barry Weeks, and David Will, a core member for nearly 25 years.

Barry and Dave only had a few weeks to sing alongside the newly added Jeremie. With Armond battling health issues and looking likely to retire, they decided it was time to move on.

In 2000, Armond released a solo album titled *Through the Years*, featuring 11 re-recorded Imperials hits with his lead vocals. These "greatest hits" reinforced the notion that Armond was winding down his career.

Meanwhile, Barry and Dave formed two-thirds of a new trio called "New Spirit." Ben Jacklin rounded out the group on tenor. Though Barry and Dave could handle lead, Dave took on that role more often, given his higher profile, which they hoped would attract fans. Dave's daughter Angela described their sound as more akin to The Imperials than traditional southern gospel.

In addition to his New Spirit duties, Barry stayed busy writing songs like "This is the Hour" (2001) and producing projects like *Light of the World* (2003). His music found its way to major TV networks, and he produced albums for Francesca Battistelli, Mandisa, Avalon, the Backstreet Boys, and more.

David Will's exit after so many years opened the door for another Morales family member to join the ranks – Armond's son Jason became the new Imperial's baritone around 1999.

**And The Imperials just kept singing…**


### 2000-2003

### Armond Morales, Jeremie Hudson, Jason Hallcox, Jason Morales, Richie Crook, Shannon Smith

#### *I was Made for This* (2002)

The foursome of Armond and Jason Morales, tenor Jeremie Hudson, and new lead singer Richie Crook worked together on the album *I Was Made for This*. It was a collaborative effort, with each member contributing their talents.

Jason Hallcox, who had previously replaced Barry Weeks, was no longer with the group when the album was released. However, he did provide some vocal contributions and even wrote a couple of tracks, "Servant Song" and "Gabriel's Lips." Jason's life was devoted to ministry, serving as a youth pastor, worship pastor, and lead pastor in addition to his work with The Imperials.

Armond took on the role of executive producer for this album, which was not unusual for him then. What was surprising, however, was that he co-wrote five of the songs with David B. Smith, a departure from his typical involvement.

Another unexpected development was that Armond's son Jason produced the record. The album notes credit the production to "Jason Morales and The Imperials," indicating a team-oriented approach to the process.

The album's sound is noteworthy in several ways. It has a pleasant, effortless listening/adult contemporary style of music. Armond showcases his vocal talents with short solos on the second and third tracks. The ninth cut, the title song "I Was Made for This," is an Armond solo from start to finish. Additionally, Jeremie Hudson's voice resembles that of Jody McBrayer of Avalon with both men capable of reaching extremely high notes.

After the release of *I Was Made for This*, Richie Crook left the group and was replaced by Shannon Smith. Shannon, a pastor's son with a strong desire to serve the Lord through music, had spent two years as a solo artist, preparing him for the role of lead singer with The Imperials, a position he would hold for several years.

The album was collaborative, with each member contributing their unique talents and perspectives, resulting in a harmonious blend of voices and styles.

The era of the original group was over... For now...

**And The Imperials just kept singing…**

# Chapter 14

## New Members/Familiar Sound

### 2003-2010

## Jeremie Hudson, Jason Morales, Shannon Smith and Ian Owens

### The Imperials (2006)
### Back to the Roots (2007)

This newly formed lineup released some excellent albums over the next few years, steadily continuing the Imperials' brand and music. Their first album, *The Imperials*, was produced by Jeffrey Teague and Steve Dady. It featured a couple of songs written by former Imperials members - "True" was penned by Billy Simon and fan favorite Jimmie Lee Sloas, and the highly talented Barry Weeks and Jody Braselton wrote "Holy & Acceptable." As a nod to their history, this new group also covered the Imperials' classic song "Big God."

Tim Holder commented, "I remember listening to it and thinking part of the album reminded me a little of NewSong, and then they covered NewSong's big hit 'Arise My Love.' They sounded similar to NewSong on part of their record, but both groups are distinct. And both of them are great."

This version of the Imperials had a pop sound with songs relying more on powerful vocals than their previous few albums. Stylistically, they were more in sync with the Imperials' music from the late 1970s to the early 1990s. An interesting thing about this release is that each song in the liner notes had an associated Scripture verse. For example, "Everything I Am" by Mark Stegall and Scott Frazier was linked to Mark 13:29-30. While not the only group to do this, it's a cool and rare touch.

117

Long-time fan Allen Stenmark's favorite song on the record was "Holy and Acceptable."

The follow-up album Back to the Roots leaned further into the group's history by covering eleven Imperials' hits from the 1960s and 1970s. This was an inspired choice since several Imperial compilation albums had been released over the years, but most focused on material from the late 70s through the 90s.

Produced by Michael Sykes and co-produced by David Ponder, *Back to the Roots* had something for every Imperials fan. It opened with the classic southern gospel four-part harmony song "Your First Day in Heaven." It featured plenty of background harmonies as the guys took turns on lead vocals for several old favorites, including some bass solos.

With these two great albums, Jeremie, Jason, Shannon, and Ian gave Imperials fans a treat. *Back to the Roots* even won "Album of the Year" from *Southern Gospel News*—while that source may seem surprising, the album did have southern gospel elements with all four voices heard simultaneously, even if the overall sound appealed more too contemporary music lovers.

This foursome produced two albums they could be genuinely proud of and were a blessing to many fans. In 2008, Shannon left to spend more time with family, taking a worship leader job at a church in Florida. He eventually joined the southern gospel trio Three Bridges with Elliott McCoy and fellow former Imperial Jeremie Hudson, who had also left the group around the same time to pursue local church ministry for a while before joining Three Bridges when the opportunity arose.

**And The Imperials just kept singing…**

## 2008-2010

**Jason Morales, Ian Owens, Scott Allen, Perry Jones**

It was a special moment when Tim Holder saw The Imperials perform live for the second time in his life in Knoxville, Tennessee. He had previously caught their show in 1984, but this second concert held extra significance. Not only was the group's lineup fantastic, but Armond Morales, the father of lead singer Jason Morales, was in attendance.

During the show, Jason shouted out to his dad from the stage and then invited Armond to join them and sing a song. It was a touching father-son moment that left a lasting impression on Tim and likely the entire audience.

While The Imperials never got to record Bryan Duncan's song "Every Father is a Son," which he wrote as a duet for Armond and Jason, the sentiment behind it resonated deeply. Eventually, Bryan recorded the tune with one of his own sons instead.

Although that particular lineup of The Imperials disbanded in 2010, the music lived on through its members. Bass singer Ian Owens stayed active by releasing a 2015 album, *Ain't Misbehavin'*. He also performed with acts like Ernie Haase and Signature Sound and the award-winning southern gospel group The Tribute Quartet.

In 2020, former Imperial's lead vocalist Scott Allen released the album *Horizon*. It featured a duet called "Angel on My Shoulder" with his old bandmate Russ Taff, making for a nostalgic reunion between the two talented singers.

So while that era of The Imperials may be in the rearview, the incredible music and cherished memories from Tim's concert experience in Knoxville still resonate strongly.

**And The Imperials just kept singing…**

## Chapter 15

## The Hawaii Imperials

## 2004

## Armond Morales, Jim Murray, Sherman Andrus, Terry Blackwood, David Will

Even though they were never officially called "The Hawaii Imperials," the group that reunited and sang together in Hawaii was a pretty special thing. It all started when Jim got an invitation to get the band back together for a reunion show in Hawaii. Armond, Sherman, and Terry were all on board, so they made it happen.

Terry was the first to return to the mainland after the reunion gig. To keep the Hawaii magic going, they brought in David Will to take Terry's spot—a repeat of history with the original Imperial lineup changes back in the day.

They kept the Hawaii vibes rolling, singing together in paradise for a while. But eventually, they all decided it was time to move back to the mainland too. Sherman was the real holdout, though - he stuck in Hawaii for four more years after the other guys had left!

That cherished reunion and Hawaiian experience struck a chord with Imperial fans worldwide. People were stoked to see them back together, even if it was just for a short time. Although that group didn't stay together for long, it planted the seed. It paved the way for Armond, Jim, and Dave to reform the Imperials, find that missing piece of the puzzle, and make their big comeback in the contemporary Christian music scene.

**And The Imperials just kept singing…**

## Chapter 16

## A Big Year for The Imperials' Music

## 2006

## Armond Morales, Jim Murray, Joe Moscheo, Terry Blackwood, Sherman Andrus

### *The Gospel Side of Elvis* (2006)

## Armond, Jim Murray, David Will, Russ Taff

### *The Lost Album* (2006

First up, we have Jeremie Hudson, Jason Morales, Shannon Smith, and Ian Owens, who formed The Imperials during a pivotal era. Interestingly, even as their album hit the shelves in 2006, other Imperials' music also reached audiences.

Let's talk about *The Gospel Side of Elvis*. It stemmed from the long-standing connection between Elvis Presley, The Imperials, and the renowned southern gospel group, the Stamps. As we've learned earlier, The Imperials served as backup vocalists for Elvis from 1969 to 1971, but their collaboration dates back to 1966 when they started recording albums together. Even after parting ways from Elvis's live performances, The Imperials continued to join him for all-night singing sessions. The Stamps then became Elvis's backup vocalists from 1972 to 1977. Both groups also participated in the "Elvis: The Concert" performances worldwide after Elvis's untimely demise.

Around 2004, an idea was sparked by a conversation between Elvis's former musical director from the 1970s, Joe Guercio, and Ed Enoch of the Stamps. They thought it would be fantastic if the Stamps and The Imperials collaborated to create an album of gospel songs that held special significance for both groups and Elvis. This collaboration was made even more meaningful by the shared history between the two groups, dating back to the 1960s when they performed at many of the same Southern Gospel venues.

The album *The Gospel Side of Elvis* wasn't just about having The Imperials perform Elvis's favorite gospel songs; it was about bringing together the specific individuals who had sung them with him. Armond, Jim, Terry Blackwood, and Joe Moscheo had all performed with Elvis. Sherman was brought in because he was singing with Armond, Jim, and Terry in Hawaii and had been friends with Elvis.

Moving on to another intriguing release, the so-called *Lost Album*, briefly mentioned earlier, was the first (unreleased) project with Russ Taff and Dave Will Era. It was finally released in 2006. Had it been available in 1976, it would have served as a nice bridge between The Imperials' sound with Sherman and Terry at the forefront and the dynamic change they would undergo with Russ and Dave. However, it wasn't the radical shift the record company sought at the time.

There are a few noteworthy points about this album for the die-hard Imperial fans (who, let's be honest, are likely the ones reading this book). Firstly, while Gary Paxton was the primary producer, Bob MacKenzie and Joe Moscheo, who had left The Imperials before Sherman and Terry, also had a hand in producing it. Secondly, David Will wrote a rare song for the album, titled "In the Same Old Fashioned Way." Although this album wasn't released in the 1970s, the song found its way onto The Imperials' *Best Of* album in 1981. As mentioned earlier, a different iteration of The Imperials would record the song a few decades later.

Although the above releases and versions of the group (in the last few chapters) may seem insignificant, nothing could be further from the truth. The Imperials' legacy lies just beneath the world stage for a season, gathering strength and resolve for their last and final push to regain their cherished ranking in the CCM marketplace.

**And The Imperials just kept singing**…

## Chapter 17

## The Classic Imperials

## 2007-2010

## Armond Morales, David Will, Jim Murray, Rick Evans, Robbie Hiner, Paul Smith

### *Standing Strong* (2008)

Through all the ups and downs, the resignations and restarts, and the loss of all the original and iconic members, it would seem that The Imperials were winding down, and that the group's legacy would be left to posterity. But wait. Here is the twist no one expected.

In 2007, Armond Morales decided he still had some music left in him, but The Imperials already had a full complement of singers. Undaunted, Armond solidified the already created "Classic Imperials." He connected with Imperial's veterans, Dave Will to sing baritone and Jim Murray to sing tenor. Armond added longtime singer and Imperials enthusiast Rick Evans on lead vocals.

Rick was intrigued when Armond called him, and coincidentally, Rick was already in Hawaii. There were a couple of complicating factors, though. One, Rick and Armond were on different islands. Two, Rick was with his wife, Debra, relaxing and enjoying the sun. So, as providence would have it, Debra got a previously unplanned day at the spa, and Rick got his meeting with Armond.

When Rick joined the group, it culminated a journey that began much earlier. When Ron Hemby left The Imperials, Rick auditioned for the group and was convinced he had made the team, but it did not work out then.

Like several of his fellow Imperials, Rick started singing in church early and wanted to continue serving the Lord that way. He gained valuable experience singing in groups from his time with the Crownsmen and the Californians.

Rick later traveled and sang with various ministries, including those of Billy Graham, Franklin Graham, Greg Laurie, and Chuck Smith. While singing for Dennis Agajanian and Billy Graham, Rick got to work with fellow vocalist Lonnie Ott, who would later join The Imperials.

Rick is not the only Christian celebrity in his family, though. Rick's wife, Debra Evans, is the author of the book *But for God: Through Broken Window Panes*, which is about shattered lives and reconciliation with God. Mentioning Debra's work emphasizes that she has a proper perspective on facing challenges. She saw the challenge Rick would face as the newest lead singer of The Imperials, and her encouragement gave Rick the peace to pursue this dream.

Rick knew that taking on the lead vocalist position previously held by legendary singers like Russ Taff, Paul Smith, and Ron Hemby would be no easy task.

Debra noted that Armond Morales was shrewd when bringing people into The Imperials, though. They had to be top-notch singers, but Armond was also interested in what else they could bring to the table. Paul Smith, for example, had incredible singing ability, but Armond recognized Paul's talent as a songwriter, too.

So, what did Rick bring to the group besides being able to sing the songs? According to Debra, "Rick is selfless. He can see down the road. He's able to make the hard choices. He puts others before himself. Integrity is a big thing for my husband. He's an incredible manager. I'm not just saying this because he's my husband. He's able to communicate."

Longtime Imperials fan Dan Ames has also appreciated what Rick has meant to the group. When asked about Rick, Dan said, "What a heart for the Lord! His heart and passion for ministry impressed me, and I realized that ministry is first, music second."

Tim Holder, who wrote this entire section, added his own thoughts: "I see Rick's unbridled enthusiasm, heart for ministry, longstanding love for The Imperials, and relational skills. This made Rick a great fit for The Imperials when Armond picked him, and still to this day."

The Imperials' journey has been a winding road filled with ups, downs, departures, and reinventions. But with passionate veterans like Rick Evans now at the helm helping to steer the ship, the legendary group's legacy continues.

The Imperials were a powerhouse in contemporary Christian music during the 2000s. They maintained a rigorous touring schedule, doing five or six shows per month across the country. Rick Evans and Dave Will shared the speaking duties, with Rick handling introductions and altar calls while Dave delivered the main message and invitation.

When she met Rick, Debra Evans was relatively new to the contemporary Christian music scene. She was amazed by the group's widespread impact, recalling, "I couldn't believe the touch that they had. Everywhere we went, people knew them. Fans would come up after concerts saying, 'I came to Christ at such and such an Imperials concert.'"

In 2008, the group recorded the album *Standing Strong*, produced by Robbie Hiner, who had also become their new tenor after Jim Murray's departure at that time. While not quite the power pop of their late '80s/early '90s heyday, the album offered a contemporary sound with country influences. Lonnie Ott said "Robbie is a pure classical tenor and a wonderful, Godly man. And musically, he was a perfectionist".

Long-time fan Phil Brown felt *Standing Strong* and its 2010 follow-up, *Still Standing*, were underrated. They were filled with great songs like "Reign," "A Place Called Heaven," "Roll the Stones," and "Days of Elijah." The latter, co-written by Armond Morales, became a hit with Rick on lead vocals. Rick's personal favorite was "The Love of God," while Debra Evans and Allen Stenmark, respectively, preferred "Reign" and "A Place Called Heaven."

2010 was also the year The Imperials were inducted into the Christian Music Hall of Fame, a separate honor from the Gospel Music Hall of Fame. Former member Russ Taff joined them onstage for an exceptional reunion performance.

For a few years after that, the "Classic" lineup of Armond, Dave, Rick, and Robbie toured together before making a significant change, even as the "younger" offshoot of the group continued performing.

**And The Imperials just kept singing**...

## Chapter 18

## The Next Step

## 2010-2017

## Armond Morales, David Will, Rick Evans, Paul Smith

### *Still Standing* (2010)
### *The Ultimate Collection* (2014)

By this time, the "younger Imperials" had disbanded, but the older version of the group was still making music and doing ministry. They dropped the "Classic" from their name and were again "The Imperials." However, Robbie Hiner's exit had left the group one man short.

The most straightforward and logical choice would have been to grab another tenor and move forward, but Rick wanted to do something bold. Armond and Dave had long talked with Rick about what a great guy Paul Smith was to have in The Imperials. He loved God, was an excellent songwriter (as stated repeatedly in this book), had a fantastic voice, and was the easiest guy to work with—he was always on time and had a good attitude.

The three men agreed that Paul should be invited back, and fortunately, he decided to follow in Dave's footsteps and return to the group. This decision proved to be a wise one.

Paul was to be the same asset to the group the second time around as he had been before. His personality, faith, and talent as a singer and songwriter continued to be pluses. Paul Mills, who had produced The Imperials' *Stir It Up* years after Paul Smith left, had the privilege of making one of the solo albums of the ex-Imperial, *Extreme Measure*. Paul Mills described Paul Smith glowingly: "Paul always had a big smile when I worked with him. He was great to work with in the studio—an amazing voice and writer. He always gave it one hundred percent when delivering a vocal performance. A producer/engineer's dream."

Debra Evans saw Paul as a tremendous blessing to The Imperials. She noted, "He loves God. Paul is a man of integrity. He has paid a tremendous price to be standing where he is. He's not a man of compromise. He LOVES his wife Denise, and he loves people. He knows how to sing. He has a trained voice, but he also has so much feeling. He sings with a lot of heart."

While they did not tour as much as The Imperials did earlier, they still spent time on the road, even taking an overseas trip to Norway. During this season, their album *Still Standing* was released in 2010. The album had a mostly pop sound, with a hint of country in some songs. Paul and Rick shared the responsibilities on lead vocals, but Dave and Armond also got their moments. The second-to-last track, "Love Speaks for Itself," featured Dave Will's last solo performance as an Imperial. And fittingly, the final cut, "Something's Wrong with the World," opened with a spoken word offering from Armond, the veteran voice of the legendary group.

There's an interesting bit of history to note in this era. Even though it was in 2014, quite a while after The Imperials' heyday, Word Records released an album called *Beginnings: Russ Taff*. The album only had Russ's name on it, but it was a collection of twelve Imperial hits where Russ was on lead vocals. It's a testament to the incredible music The Imperials made back then.

Also in 2014, the record company released another compilation called *Imperials: The Ultimate Collection*. This one had songs from their *Sail On* album up through *Free the Fire*. The record company called many of their "Best Of" releases "*The Ultimate Collection*" then. Still, it was a misnomer for The Imperials because their *Legacy* album had a bigger collection of songs from that same period.

Fast forward to around 2015, and The Imperials were part of this huge event that brought together Christian artists from several decades to perform condensed versions of their biggest hits - 45 songs in total! It was televised, released on DVD, and as a double CD called *We Will Stand*. That name was inspired by the hit Russ Taff song, the second-to-last track on the album. There was also a book released with the same name by Stan Moser to tie in with the whole project.

For their part, The Imperials performed "Trumpet of Jesus," and then Michael W. Smith and Steven Curtis Chapman joined them on "Praise the Lord." Interestingly, the four Imperial guys on stage were Armond, Jim, Russ, and Dave Will. Rick was there supporting them, but he didn't perform.

So on this *We Will Stand* album, you had The Imperials sharing the bill with Christian music legends like Amy Grant, Michael W. Smith, Steven Curtis Chapman, Petra, Larnelle Harris, Steve Green, 4Him, and more. It was a real Who's Who. Bonnie Keen from First Call, who was there, called it "a lovefest." Just an amazing gathering of talent all on one huge project.

**And The Imperials just kept singing…**

## 2018-2021

### Armond Morales, David Will, Rick Evans, Paul Smith, Lonnie Ott, Michael Schlee, Ron Hemby

As the surviving legacy of The Imperials continued, in 2018, Dave Will had some health issues and again had to leave The Imperials. The group would deeply miss his singing and extraordinary abilities to fix just about anything that needed fixing, but they would especially miss his outstanding character and warm presence.

Debra Evans, Rick's wife, got to know Dave well when Rick joined The Imperials. Rick and Debra moved to

130

Nashville and lived with the Wills for a while. Debra fondly recalled, "He had a wonderful, compassionate heart. He loved to sing for the Lord. He was there for God. He loved people. David was truly special. He just loved God." She also marveled at his dedicated study of the Bible.

Lonnie Ott, a seasoned vocalist with a long history of working with Rick, replaced David Will as the group's baritone singer. As you may recall, Lonnie and Rick had previously sung together in the Billy Graham and Franklin Graham Crusades as part of the Dennis Agajanian Band. They were also part of the Harvest Crusades with Pastor Greg Laurie.

Lonnie was thrilled to work again with his "true brother in Christ" Rick. As Lonnie put it, "We're like family."

Lonnie's career in the music business spanned decades, starting at the tender age of six when he first sang on a record. He toured with his parents as part of the Ott Trio and vividly remembers performing at the same concert as The Imperials when he was just a kid.

Lonnie particularly relished singing so many of the classic Imperials songs he grew up admiring. Fan favorites like "No Shortage" and "Gospel Ship" were among his highlights.

Later in 2018, the legendary Armond Morales retired from The Imperials—this time for good. His final appearance with the group was a poignant appearance on the Huckabee Show, where the host warmly credited The Imperials with providing the soundtrack for his life. The group performed their signature hit "The Love of God," which opened with an Armond solo and featured Rick on the second verse. Then Mike Huckabee treated his viewers even more, as this quartet of Imperials was joined by esteemed alums Russ Taff and Jim Murray for a rousing medley of songs. Lonnie Ott was also there to sing, along with Robbie Hiner, who filled in because Paul Smith could not attend.

For Lonnie, the chance to perform with Armond, Jim, and Russ was an unparalleled blessing. As he later reflected, "I don't get star-struck, but I told them what an honor it was to get to work with them." Lonnie added that other than working with Billy Graham, singing with Armond, Jim, and Russ was his life's most awesome professional experience.

Jeffrey Benward summed up the thoughts of countless Imperial fans when he asked rhetorically, "Who can sing bass like Armond Morales?"

In the wake of Armond's retirement, the group took some well-deserved time off. Even when they did start performing again, they didn't do much at first. Armond had left immensely big shoes to fill, not just musically—he embodied The Imperials in many ways. Pausing the group for a season seemed appropriate to honor his legendary impact.

As The Imperials navigated lineup changes, Michael Schlee stepped in as the new bass singer following Armond's departure. Lonnie fondly described Michael as "a great friend and mentor. He loves the Lord." With a background in southern gospel, Michael brought a traditional bass singing style to the group.

During this era, Rick, Lonnie, Paul, and Michael faced limitations on touring due to the COVID-19 pandemic. However, they made a memorable trip to Norway, where they had the opportunity to perform multiple times. They still laugh about a luggage mishap, with some bags never making it to Norway. Michael looked forward to rocking his "blue Swede" shoes, an inside joke among the group members.

In 2021, a significant change occurred when Michael Schlee left the group. Instead of replacing him with another bass singer, Rick, who also served as the group's manager in addition to being one of its members, had a different idea in mind. Rick had previously worked with Ron Hemby on a project involving The Imperials that didn't come to fruition. Still, during that time, Ron expressed his willingness to help Rick or The Imperials in any way possible. Recognizing Ron's extraordinary talent, positive spirit, and sense of humor, Rick and Paul decided to bring Ron back into the group.

With this move, Lonnie began singing the bass parts, and the group now had three legitimate lead singers. Having three front men in a four-person group could have been disastrous, but they were so talented and humble that it worked seamlessly.

Bonnie Keen, one of the many impressed by Ron Hemby as a person and a vocalist, shared her thoughts on the man. "Ron is one of those vocalists with a unique, God-given talent. He has a quintessential sound," she said.

Bonnie has known Ron well since they and several others have performed together in the Eaglemaniacs for ten years. When talking about Ron, Bonnie said, "He is so humble. He has no airs. He's just a joy to be around—very endearing."

Looking back on those days with The Imperials, Lonnie enjoyed the good humor and laughter shared among the guys. However, there was more than just that. There were moments like a Christmas concert in Fresno, where Ron sang lead on "Immanuel," and the guys joined in on the harmonies. They were not focused on making a hit song or wowing the crowd; they were worshiping and leading in worship. As Lonnie said, "Our goal was to get the music to melt their hearts and minister to them."

**And The Imperials just kept singing**…

## Chapter 19

## The Final Frontier

## 2022-Present

## Rick Evans, Paul Smith, Ron Hemby, Rod Fletcher

### *Blessed* (2023)

As Lonnie Ott departed the group, a fresh talent joined the ranks – Rod Fletcher, who would be the last bass singer for the Imperials. Rod's musical journey had taken him to incredible heights, including performing at the prestigious Grand Ole Opry since 1996. Eventually, he became the leader of the background vocalists there. Before that, Rod was a member of Disney's Voices of Liberty, a renowned ensemble that graces the American Adventure Pavilion at EPCOT in Walt Disney World. Throughout his illustrious career, Rod has collaborated with luminaries like Michael Omartian, Sandi Patty, Faith Hill, Garth Brooks, and numerous others.

Larry Hall, who occasionally played in the band for The Imperials on the road over the years, holds Rod in high esteem as a person and singer. In Larry's words, "He's a super nice guy, and a consummate professional. He's an incredible bass singer—one of Nashville's first-call bass singers."

While Rod is the newest addition to the current lineup, he has been an ardent fan of the Imperials for years. The first Imperials song he heard was the Russ Taff-led rocker "Water Grave," which opened their album *Sail On*. Little did Rod know then that he would one day become part of this legendary group.

Producer Tom Reeves inadvertently paved the way for Rod's inclusion. Tom invited Rod to the studio to lend his vocals to a track being recorded for the album *Blessed*. Unbeknownst to Rod, the song was a recut of The Imperials' classic "I'm Forgiven." Upon learning that the group needed a bass singer, Rod expressed his interest, and soon enough, Tom Reeves called Rick, securing Rod's place in the lineup.

Interestingly, Tom's wife, Peggy, had initially advocated for Rod's involvement. As Tom recalls, "She suggested that Rod come in and sing on 'I'm Forgiven.' I said, 'Yes, he would be perfect for the session.' She replied, 'He would be perfect for the group!' She was more than right!"

When asked about joining a group with such a rich history and legacy, and what it was like to be part of a quartet with three members who had been part of that history for so many years, Rod spoke of how seamlessly the transition had been. "They made me feel like I'm not an outsider. It was pretty remarkable how quickly it gelled," he said.

According to Rod, the group's dynamic is incredibly positive. "Rick laughs every time we're on the phone together. Ron has a phenomenal sense of humor. They all do. They love to laugh."

One burden Rod did not place on himself was the pressure of trying to emulate the legendary Armond Morales. "I don't have to be him. My voice isn't like his. He has a lot more bass than I do. I'm a baritone/bass," Rod humbly acknowledged.

However, Rod's self-assessment of his voice in comparison to Armond's is not universally shared. Debra Evans found Rod's singing to be "a pleasant surprise. When he opened his mouth, it was like listening to Armond Morales. I've never heard a bass singer who sounded so much like Armond."

In late 2023, The Imperials released *Blessed*, a mini-album that seamlessly blended old classics and new songs, showcasing the group's enduring talent. They kicked things off with fan favorites "No Shortage" from the Andrus and Blackwood era, and "I'm Forgiven," penned by Michael Omartian and others during Russ Taff's time with the group. Next up was "Not to Us, O Lord," a collaboration between lyricist Paul Smith and composer Michael W. Smith. These beloved tracks were followed by fresh material, including the song "Blessed" by Paul Smith and Jenny Boyd and the album's closing number, "The Way."

Reflecting on the song "Blessed," Phil Brown called it "a very powerful song for our times." Clearly thrilled with the new release, Dan Ames exclaimed, "I love it! I'm thankful they're keeping that spirit alive. And I love that harmony."

The album was produced by Tom Reeves, a former drummer for The Imperials, and Paul Smith. With their intimate familiarity with the group's signature sound from years past and their modern sensibilities, Tom and Paul crafted a production that honored the legacy while keeping things fresh. Rod believed Tom's long history with the band was a definite asset for the project. As mentioned earlier, Rod held Paul's musicality in high regard from his initial stint with the group.

At this stage, The Imperials are far from simply coasting on nostalgia. With Rick, Paul, and Ron still delivering powerhouse lead vocals, and Rod's continued performances at the Grand Ole Opry underscoring his remarkable pipes, there's too much talent in this lineup to merely rest on their laurels.

Ministry remains the driving force behind The Imperials' endeavors. According to Rick, "We're trying to reach the church now. We desire to work with churches to help bridge the gap between the current and next generations." These days, when The Imperials hit the road, they perform at churches. Rick has served as a pastor at multiple churches, and both Paul and Ron have extended experience as worship pastors. They intimately understand the challenges and opportunities involved in working within church communities.

Thanks to their more relaxed touring schedule, the guys enjoy pursuing other projects flexibly. Ron lends his vocals to the Eaglemaniacs, a group dedicated to performing the music of the Eagles and Don Henley, alongside fellow musicians Tom (Ron's brother), Bonnie Keen, and Larry Hall and others. Rick manages the Imperials while also running a business in Florida. Rod leads the band at the iconic Grand Ole Opry, while Paul is a voice teacher and vocal coach in Texas.

Slower pace or not, The Imperials remain committed to their core mission: creating music that glorifies the Lord and using that music as a ministry to touch lives. This "Final Frontier" is The Imperials' "Sail On" move in their more than 60-year legacy (sorry, couldn't resist the pun). Paul, Rick, and Ron agree that this is their last major push with the group. They aim to establish a legacy for the next generation before passing the torch. No one knows how far or how long it will go, but after over 60 years, they've stopped asking that question and are simply pressing on.

The final thought: The Imperials are always looking for new ways to expand the footprint. So, you can expect the unexpected. But, for now, Paul Smith, Rick Evans, Ron Hemby, and Rod Fletcher are the Imperials and are hopefully coming to town near you.

**And The Imperials just keep singing…**

### Former Imperials Today

In 2023, Jim Murray's induction into the Tri-State Hall of Fame was a momentous occasion. The Tri-State region comprises Tennessee, Alabama, and Georgia, and being recognized across this area was a significant achievement. However, the true highlights for Jim are his connections with people over the years. "When folks tell me about a song I sang or a 'hello' I gave them, those are the real highlights," he shared. "When people reach out with a note or story, it means the world to me. Being able to impact people's lives and make an eternal difference - that's what it's all about."

Jim's wife, Brenda Murray, has been actively sharing memories and stories from The Imperials' journey on social media, a tremendous blessing for longtime fans. As of 2024, Jim and Brenda continue to perform Elvis Concerts, featuring an Elvis impersonator and several musicians who performed with the King himself.

Jim Murray, Sherman Andrus, and Terry Blackwood maintain websites selling albums from their years with The Imperials and various other projects. In 2024, Jim and Terry frequently sang and streamed directly to family and friends through social media platforms.

Jimmie Lee Sloas and Barry Weeks remained in high demand in the music business, working with various top artists throughout this period.

In 2025, Russ Taff had two new projects to be proud of. One was a recently produced, limited-release Christmas album produced by Larry Hall, and the other was an album of cover songs delivered in a blues style, entitled *Cover Story*. Russ and his wife, Tori, also continue to host the annual Bell Buckle Weekend every fall, gathering musical talent over the years like Imperials alums Ron Hemby, James Hollihan, Larry Hall, and other Christian artists, and making music for Russ's fans. The event's name was derived from its location - Bell Buckle, Tennessee.

Jeremie Hudson sang with the Christian country group Texas Star through the end of 2024, continuing to use his voice for the Lord.

Ian Owens remained a part of the Tribute Quartet in 2025.

After leaving The Imperials in 2022, Lonnie Ott performed occasionally with Dennis Agajanian.

During this time, Shannon Smith was a worship leader, author, and public speaker.

In 2025, Brian Comeaux continued serving as the lead pastor of a church in Canada.

## The Imperials Band and Support Staff

One critical and often overlooked component of The Imperials is the impact of all the incredible band members and staff who were a critical part of the family.

It is clear that The Imperials attracted some of the best musicians of each era to serve as their band members. From songwriters and arrangers to session musicians, engineers, and producers, most went on to successful full-time careers in the music industry.

These unsung heroes were charged with being a part of the live concerts that drove The Imperials. They sat on the bus into the early morning hours discussing ways to improve the audience experience and planning how to deliver live versions of the studio recordings.

Armond Morales always had an eye for those who would fit The Imperials' makeup. Below is a sampling of Armond's hires who passed through the group's ranks—a "Who's Who" list of world class musicians.

Guitarists: James Hollihan, Tom Hemby, Brian Wooten, and Tim Norris.

Bass players: Tom Hemby, James Hollihan, Jackie Street, Jimmie Lee Sloas, Chad Watson, and Victor Caldwell.

Keyboardists: Joe Moscheo, Steve McElyea, Bill George, Dick Tunney, Boh Cooper, Tim Akers, Mark Douthit (also on sax), Dennis Patton, Kevin Salyer, and Larry Hall.

Drummers: Mike Kinard, Tom Reeves, Steve Brewster, and Brian Fullen.

There were many more who will never be forgotten, as they helped make The Imperials' live events a special moment in history.

As The Imperials' ministry grew through the years, they required more and more support staff on and off the road. Notable hires include Manager Larry Young, Merchandise Manager Wayne McKeegan, Front of House Mixer Leroy Patch, Lighting Director Al Hornung, and Administrative Assistant Lori Phelps. There were several bus and semi-truck drivers (in addition to the various singers and band members who took turns behind the wheel): Randy Turley, Byron Hillesland, Ed Suey, Jim Peacock, Roy Atkins, and Mike Gibbons.

All the above people and many others played key roles in the music and ministry of The Imperials.
**And The Imperials team just keeps serving**...

## Hit Songs Through the Years

### Song (Lead Vocals) Writer(s) Album Release Date

1. "Sweet, Sweet Spirit," (Jim Murray, et al), Doris Akers, *Love is the Thing*, 1969
2. "The First Day in Heaven," (Roger Wiles, et all), Stuart Hamblen, *Gospel's Alive and Well*, 1970
3. "Give Them All to Jesus," (Terry Blackwood), Bob Benson, Phil Johnson, *No Shortage*, 1975
4. "No Shortage," (Terry Blackwood, Sherman Andrus), Gary S. Paxton, *No Shortage*, 1975
5. "I just Came to Praise the Lord," (Sherman Andrus), Wayne Romero, *No Shortage*, 1975
6. "Sail On," (Jim Murray), Chris Christian, *Sail On*, 1977
7. "Bread on the Water," (David Will, Jim Murray, Armond Morales), Bill Grine, Janny Grine, *Sail On*, 1977
8. "Water Grave," (Russ Taff) Steve Chapman, *Sail On*, 1977
9. "The Old Gospel Ship," (David Will), Mylon Lefevre, *Imperials Live*, 1978
10. "Praise the Lord," (Russ Taff), Brown Bannister, Mike Hudson, *Heed the Call*, 1979
11. "Oh Buddha," (Russ Taff), Mark Farrow, *Heed the Call*, 1979
12. "Heed the Call," (Jim Murray), Chris Christian, *Heed the Call*, 1979
13. "Let Jesus Do it for You," (Russ Taff), Steven Ferguson, *Heed the Call*, 1979
14. "Living Without Your Love," (Jim Murray), Tom Hemby *One More Song for You*, 1979

15. "One More Song for You," (David Will), Stormie Omartian, Michael Omartian, *One More Song for You*, 1979
16. "I'm Forgiven," (Russ Taff), Michael Omartian, Bruce Hibbard, Hadley Hockensmith, *One More Song for You*, 1979
17. "Higher Power," (Russ Taff), Danny Correll, *One More Song for You*, 1979
18. "Closer Than Ever," (Russ Taff), Stormie Omartian, Michael Omartian, *One More Song for You*, 1979
19. "Eagle Song," (Russ Taff) Tori Taff, Russ Taff, *One More Song for You*, 1979
20. "The Trumpet of Jesus," (Russ Taff), Stormie Omartian, Michael Omartian, *Priority*, 1980
21. "Any Good Time at All," (Russ Taff), Stormie Omartian, Michael Omartian, *Priority*, 1980
22. "Finish What You Started," (Russ Taff), Russ Taff, Tori Taff, Michael Omartian, *Priority*, 1980
23. "I'd Rather Believe in You," (Jim Murray), Michael Omartian, Stormie Omartian, *Priority*, 1980
24. "Be Still My Soul," (Russ Taff), Russ Taff, Tori Taff, *Priority*, 1980
25. "Because of Who You Are," (David Will), Billy Smiley, Bob Farell, *Stand by the Power*, 1982
26. "Stand by the Power," (Paul Smith), Paul Smith, John Rosasco, *Stand by the Power*, 1982
27. "Lord of the Harvest," (Jim Murray), Paul Smith, James Newton Howard, *Stand by the Power*, 1982
28. "In the Promised Land," (Paul Smith), Chris Eaton, *Let the Wind Blow*, 1985
29. "Not to Us, O Lord," (four part), Paul Smith, Michael W. Smith, *Let the Wind Blow*, 1985

30. "Let the Wind Blow," (Paul Smith), David C. Martin, Phil Naish, *Let the Wind Blow*, 1985

31. "Wings of Love," (Ron Hemby), Keith Thomas, Paul Smith, *This Year's Model*, 1987

32. "Power of, God," (Ron Hemby), Ron Hemby, Tom Hemby *This Year's Model*, 1987

33. "Devoted to You," (Ron Hemby), Ron Hemby, Stephen Bashaw, *This Year's Model*, 1987

34. "Free the Fire in Me," (Ron Hemby), Michael Omartian, Stormie Omartian, *Free the Fire*, 1988

35. "The Boss," (Jimmie Lee Sloas), Jimmie Lee Sloas, *Free the Fire*, 1988

36. "Big Ball Turning," (David Robertson), Butch Stewart, Brenda Blonski *Love's Still Changing Hearts*, 1990

37. "It's Gonna be Alright," (Ron Hemby), Ron Hemby *Love's Still Changing Hearts*, 1990

38. "It's Raining Again," (David Robertson), David Robertson, *Love's Still Changing Hearts*, 1990

39. "Come Into My Life," (Ron Hemby), Paul Chiten, Pamela Philips-Oland, *Love's Still Changing Hearts*, 1990

40. "Taking Your Love for Granted," (Jonathan Hildreth), David Raynor, Kenny Lamar, Michael Peterson, *Stir It Up*, 1992

41. "A Place Called Heaven," (Rick Evans), Armond Morales, Kevin M. Wicker, *Standing Strong*, 2008

42. "We've Got a Great Big Wonderful God," (Jeremie Hudson, Shannon Smith, Jason Morales, and Ian Owens), Tim Spencer, *Back to the Roots*, 2008

43. "All That Matters to the Lord," (Jason Morales), Marty Funderburk, Twila McBride-Labar, *Back to the Roots*, 2008

44. "No More Looking Over My Shoulder," (Rick Evans), Michael Peterson, *Still Standing*, 2010

**In Memory Of**

Jason Hallcox—April 9, 2025

Jake Hess—January 4, 2004

Jonathan Pierce Hildreth—May 9, 2020

Gary McSpadden—April 15, 2020

Armond Morales—December 5, 2022

Pam Morales-Dietz—August 27, 2005

Joe Moscheo—January 11, 2016

Sherrill "Shaun" Nielsen—December 10, 2010

Henry Slaughter—November 13, 2020

David Will—March 4, 2022

## Interviews

The authors would like to thank the following individuals for being willing to be interviewed for this project:

### Members of The Imperials

Sherman Andrus, Terry Blackwood, Rod Fletcher, Ron Hemby, Jim Murray, Lonnie Ott, Paul Smith, Danny Ward, and Barry Weeks

### Musicians and Producers

Chris Christian, Larry Hall, Tom Hemby, James Hollihan Jr., Neal Joseph, Paul Mills, Michael Omartian, Tom Reeves, Bill Schnee, Keith Thomas, and Dick Tunney

### Other Christian Singers

Lisa Bevill, Jeoffrey Benward, Steven Curtis Chapman, Andy Chrisman (of 4Him), Bryan Duncan, Bonnie Keen (of First Call), Kelli Reisen, and Melodie Tunney (of Truth and First Call)

### Music Executives, Family Members, and Fans

Dan Ames, Bill Anderson, Greg Austin, Phil Brown, Debra Evans, Chris Hauser, Steve Krampitz, Jay McCluskey, Brenda Murray, Stan Moser, Allan Stenmark, Jeff Walker, and Michelle Younkman

## Bibliography

Andrus, Sherman. *My Story! His Song! Blessed!* Bloomington, IN: WestBow Press, 2021.

Christian, Chris with Bill Ireland. *A Grandmother's Prayer: Moments in a Music Life.* Travelers Rest, SC: True Potential, 2018.

Moscheo, Joe. *The Gospel Side of Elvis.* New York: Center Street, 2007.

Moser, Stan. *We Will Stand.* Brentwood, TN: Christian Music United, 2015.

Taff, Russ, Tori Taff, and Mark Smeby. *I Still Believe.* Nashville: Post Hill Press, 2019

Taff, Tori, et al. *100 Greatest Songs in Christian Music.* Brentwood, TN: Integrity Publishers, 2006.

**Partial List of Other Books by Timothy D. Holder**

*Forged in Fire and Hope: The Faith of Five Presidents*

*Feeling the Squeeze: Success Through Adversity*

*Devotions for a New Day*
Coauthored with Jill Holder

*Devotions with Presidents*

# Acknowledgements

## Rick L. Evans

My dearest love, Debra: You are the light of my life. Without your unwavering love and support, my life would be completely different. Thank you from the bottom of my heart for walking by my side through all these years, as we've navigated the path that God set before us. Words cannot fully express how deeply I love you.

To Paul and Denise Smith for their unwavering support as we work to safeguard the enduring legacy of The Imperials for future generations. Your steadfast presence by our side means everything as we strive to preserve this CCM treasure.

This book wouldn't have been possible without the invaluable contributions of Tim Holder. His partnership, patience, professionalism, and extraordinary talent as a writer were the instruments God used to bring these words to life. I'm deeply grateful for his friendship, dedication, and skill in guiding in this process.

To Everett Evans, Dennis Agajanian, Lonnie Ott, Franklin Graham, Pastor Greg Laurie, Pastor Chuck Smith, and all the other amazing individuals who helped nurture the gift that God gave me. Their guidance and support allowed me to develop the strength and resilience needed to withstand the challenges of my calling. Without their mentorship, I wouldn't be where I am today.

To my Lord and Savior, Jesus Christ, for every Saving Grace and Mercy.

## Timothy D. Holder

I would like to thank Jill for her love, support, encouragement, creativity, and good ideas. I am also very appreciative of her for listening to me talk so much about this project along the way. She is involved in almost everything I do, and I am continually impressed by her sharp mind, her insight, her ability to figure out how to make things better, and her tender heart. Her vision for the cover design was great. I love her so very much.

Greg Austin's enthusiasm for the idea of this book was a blessing to me.

I appreciated Jennifer Blackwood's belief that I could move this project from zero to one. Her encouragement came at the perfect time—it was right before doors began opening.

Rick Evans's enthusiasm, kindness, energy, and encyclopedic knowledge of The Imperials were all amazing. His kindness and friendship have been an added blessing.

Jeff Bohanan and Jonathan Hodge are both men of great wisdom. When I succeed at something big—like writing or cowriting a book—I think about how these two men, along with Jill, have given me tools to figure out how to move forward professionally, take next steps, and accomplish new and bigger things.

Jessica Martin's intelligence and talent as an editor have made this book something better than it would otherwise have been. She is excellent at both the art and science of writing. I literally marveled at her feedback. She is a blessing.

I would again like to thank, as we did above in our section on interviews, those individuals who shared their time and insights. It was such a blessing and so much fun to talk with each of you.

I am grateful to Rick, Paul Smith, Ron Hemby, Barry Weeks, Jim and Brenda Murray, and Steve Krampitz for sharing their pictures of the group over the years. The pictures of the current group on the front and back of the book were provided by Philip G. Brown Photography. Phil did a great job.

To the Author of all things, I am eternally thankful. I will be grateful for eternity.

## Author Bios

### Rick L. Evans

Rick Evans, the CEO and manager of The Imperials, has dedicated his life to full-time ministry since the age of 22. He joined The Imperials almost 20 years ago and has been an integral part of the group since then. Previously, Evans spent 13 years as a member of the Dennis Agajanian Band and served as a featured team member at the Franklin Graham Crusades. His extensive experience includes touring globally with prominent ministries such as Harvest Crusades (Greg Laurie), Promise Keepers, and Billy Graham.

With a degree in Human Development, Evans leverages his education and expertise to counsel, consult, and teach the Body of Christ and organizations aimed at reaching beyond traditional boundaries. He shares a ministry with his wife, Debra Evans, who is a keynote speaker. Debra's ministry focuses on healing, restoration, and reconciliation, encouraging individuals to overcome their past and embrace God's restorative power.

In addition to his other roles, Rick Evans serves as a pastor, teacher, consultant, and counselor. He is dedicated to developing Christ-centered leaders with effective ministry skills and resources. Through "Impact Consulting," Evans provides Christ-centered consulting services to churches and ministry-based organizations, helping them achieve their goals and maximize their impact.

### Timothy D. Holder

Tim is the author of twenty books, a history professor, a public speaker, and an actor. His books tend to be about faith, presidents, or both. He teaches online for Liberty University and Walters State Community College. He speaks forty to fifty times a year to civic groups, schools, and churches. He also does pulpit supply preaching. He has acted in movies, on television, and in commercials, usually with his wife, Jill Holder, an actress and producer. They live in Knoxville, Tennessee. Tim is the stepfather of five kids.

Evans and Holder

www.ingramcontent.com/pod-product-compliance
Lightning Source LLC
Chambersburg PA
CBHW060350090426
42734CB00011B/2093